THE NEW TESTAMENT IS YOU

L. Emerson Ferrell

Voice of The Light Ministries

THE NEW TESTAMENT IS YOU

©**L. Emerson Ferrell**
1st Edition, 2025

COPYRIGHT

All rights reserved. This publication may not be reproduced or transmitted in any form or any means, filed in an electronic system nor transmitted in any electronic, mechanical way including photocopying, recording or by any information storage retrieval system, or in any other manner (including audiobooks), without the previous written permission of the author.

All Scripture quotations, unless indicated otherwise, have been taken from the New King James Version (NKJV) © 1982 by Thomas Nelson Inc., used by permission. All rights reserved.

Category: Reformation
Published by: Voice of The Light Ministries / U.S.A.
Cover Design: Ana Méndez Ferrell
Layout Design :   Andrea Jaramillo

Printed in The United States of America

www.voiceofthelight.com

Voice of The Light Ministries - P. O. Box 3418 Ponte Vedra Florida, 32004 / U.S.A.

ISBN: 978-1-944681-72-2

CONTENTS

7		**INTRODUCTION**
13	CHAPTER 1	**OUR ORIGIN IS IMAGELESS**
21	CHAPTER 2	**BETWEEN DIMENSIONS**
31	CHAPTER 3	**HYPNOTIC PROGRAMMING**
39	CHAPTER 4	**SPIRITUALLY PHYSICAL**
47	CHAPTER 5	**DIVINE TRANSFUSION**
55	CHAPTER 6	**WHAT DO YOU BELIEVE AND WHY?**
73	CHAPTER 7	**MONEY AND IMAGINATION**

81	CHAPTER 8	**QUANTUM SPEAK**
99	CHAPTER 9	**DOCTRINES BEWITCH**
113	CHAPTER 10	**THE ANTI-CHRIST SPIRIT**
127	CHAPTER 11	**RESONANCE OF BABYLON**
137	CHAPTER 12	**THE BIBLE WITHOUT DIVISION**
155	CHAPTER 13	**COVENANTS**
189	CHAPTER 14	**FAITH AND BELIEVE**
209	CONCLUSION	**YOU ARE THE NEW TESTAMENT**

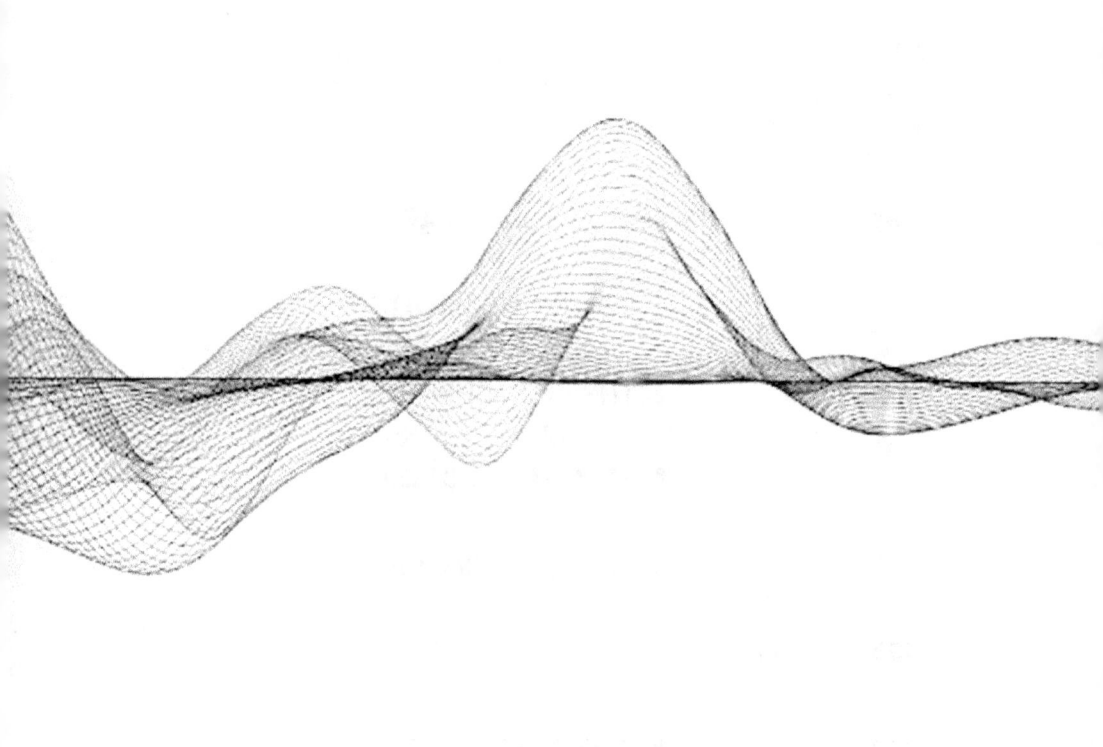

INTRODUCTION

This book is written for those who know God is their Father and have genuinely experienced Christ's love. Moreover, they are sincerely interested in discovering life changing revelations from the Holy Spirit by their searching the scriptures without being judged for their actions or ideas that may be different from the mainstream churches.

The first time my parents took me to a church, I was given a Bible and told to believe every verse because it was God's word. Well, of course, I assumed they knew what they were talking about, so I took them at their word and never questioned it or the interpretations.

It was not until I began to read the book that I discovered how difficult it was to understand. My response, like so many others, was to depend on doctrines, orthodoxies, and religion to "explain" what the Bible "really means."

The book you're holding in your hand contains the keys that, when placed in the right lock, will unveil pictures, lights, sounds, and words from the spiritual realm that were placed there for you alone to experience.

But it is not just another experience that leaves you wanting another feeling or emotion. This interaction with the divine changes your mindset from believing in a future heaven to living it now. Why? Because as you will discover, "the image" you recognize by your senses hides the mysteries you seek, which is the kingdom Jesus said to find first.

> **But seek ye first His kingdom,** and His righteousness; and all these things shall be added unto you.
>
> Matthew 6:33 NKJV

Most questions extremely relevant among people going to churches remain unanswered largely because of the disconnect between the Bible they read and the Bible they are taught. This was my experience for years and is a contributing factor to my never-ending journey to receive directly from the source, Christ Himself.

It was not until The Spirit explained to me that His Bible was written in my spirit before I was flesh that I discovered I was His New Testament, not the letters in the Bible I was reading. In other words, my origin was in Him, which eliminated my need to make a covenant with anything in the physical world.

INTRODUCTION

> *Praise the God and Father of our Lord Jesus Christ! Through Christ, God **has blessed us with every spiritual blessing** that heaven has to offer. **Before the creation of the world, He chose us through Christ** to be holy and perfect in His presence.*
>
> Ephesians 1:3-4 GWT

That verse became an earthquake inside me, shattering all the fear and doubt that kept me bound to religion's doctrinal lies. You will experience this freedom as you study this material. This isn't a book written for information; it is a mirror that will show you who you are and where you came from.

The power of who we are as God's creation is miraculous. Just like a child learning to crawl, walk, and run, it requires never being satisfied with our current position or condition. That means adamantly refusing to let comfort and predictability hypnotize you into believing you have arrived because of a doctrine or denominational teaching.

This book will reveal your position in your Father beyond the limited dimensional thinking we've been conditioned to accept as real. My life changed dramatically, and so will yours after you understand that our responses to the physical world perpetuate our current condition as flesh and blood. The simple steps you learn from this material will not only change your life but also pull back the curtains to make "the invisible" visible.

There's absolutely nothing wrong with you or your current situation that your beliefs and perceptions can't transform. I truly believe that our current understanding of Christianity has been influenced by the way we view the Bible, which is often seen as just the Old and New Testaments. If we were taught the Bible through the power of God's Covenants, we would uncover the divine path back to Oneness with our Father.

God completed His covenants with His various servants, which we will discuss in the book, to assure you and me that we could individually make a covenant with Christ at His resurrection. Jesus finished His work, and now He has extended His covenant to you personally.

Nothing is more important than our personal covenant with the resurrected Christ. This is both the purpose of this book and provides the deliverance you desperately need. This covenant is like no other because it was personally designed for your wholeness in Him.

This is unlike any other book you will read, as it is not linear but multidimensional. In other words, information will become impartation as you learn to observe your conditioned response to the visible dimension. The reason for our condition is because of our attention to this dimension.

Reminding you of that condition is why several scriptures are repeated throughout the book.

Our condition today is temporary, but His covenant is eternal because in Him, nothing is as it appears, and what will be has been waiting on you. However, you already know that, and this book serves as confirmation.

My limited knowledge of the risen Christ has led me to a place of profound wonder that surpasses my thoughts and imagination, and it is from this place that I convey my current level of understanding. I sincerely hope that for everyone reading this book, each minute spent studying it will blossom into years of joy and remarkable discoveries.

I am confident that after studying this book, your life will never be the same because it will provide the necessary revelation to expand your awareness to the fabulous journey ahead.

My suggestion is to avoid dwelling on what is unclear or irrelevant to you at this moment, as God expands and reinforces our foundations before revealing deeper truths. What exists today will remain until our spirit remembers it; this is similar to what some call déjà vu.

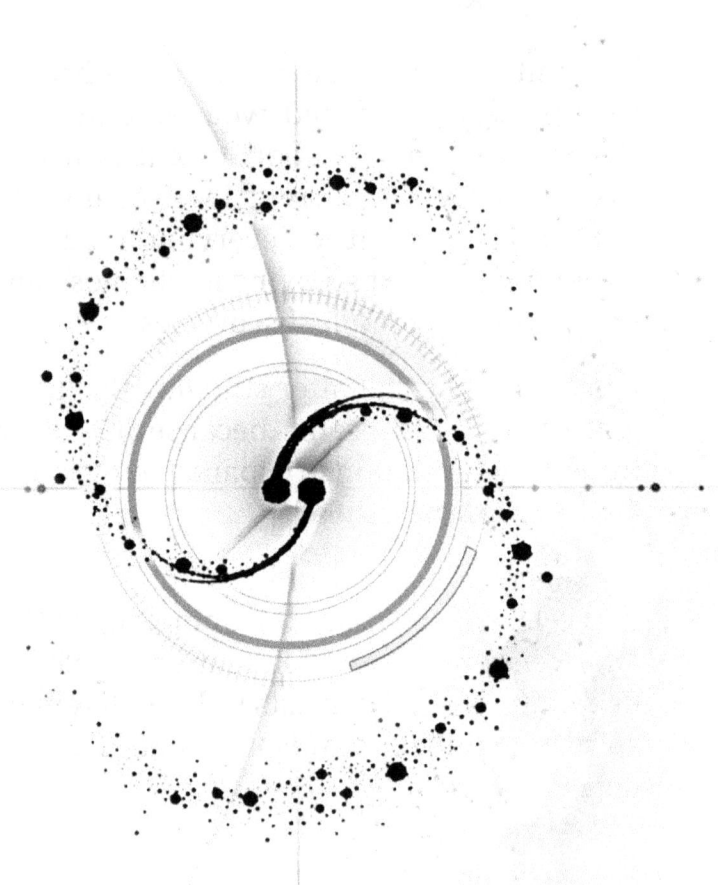

CHAPTER 1

OUR ORIGIN IS IMAGELESS

A recurring theme in this journey emphasizes the necessity of reminding ourselves that we are spiritual beings. This isn't merely an idea but a fundamental truth, which becomes particularly difficult to accept during physical pain. Our heightened sensitivity to discomfort makes it the fastest route to forgetting our spiritual nature and begin focusing on the material realm.

There exists no magic formula to eradicate physical pain; however, I have employed a method that mitigates its overwhelming capacity to capture my attention. Worship serves as the sole power that liberates me physically from its grasp. The longer my voice resonates in harmony with His love, the further I distance myself from my physical form, embracing His imageless design.

Focus on these scriptures to elevate your default frequency and combat voices reminding you of your physical image and failures.

> *God is Spirit.*
> John 4:24 NKJ

> *Then God said, "Let Us make man in Our image, according to Our likeness."*
> Genesis 1:26 NKJ

The scripture explicitly states that man was created in the image and likeness of God, who is Spirit. This implies that "man" is a spirit lacking a physical or material form within this dimension.

This is one of those scriptures that render our brain helpless because it has no memory of a spirit. If we were made in the image of a fish or a gorilla, our brain would immediately form a picture that resembles those words. This underlines the reason communication must be in the form of frequency and not words.

The Bible begins immediately with concepts that are as foreign to our way of thinking and believing as today's news headlines describing non-human beings flying UFOs.

Upon further examination, we must ultimately conclude that a distinctly different mentality is necessary to fully comprehend our miraculous origins. Furthermore, we acknowledge that our current linguistic capabilities fall short in adequately articulating the nature of the spiritual realm.

This illustrates why humanity relies on scientific branches to make sense of the unknown, using language and tools that are inherently constrained by this dimension. Thus, we continue to depend on this "limited dimension" for answers to questions that originate from beyond it. However, we will come to realize that we are born into this dimension with those answers concealed within our spirit.

Many overlook the miraculous and God's role as the Creator to evade their fears. Acknowledging our reliance on science and the wisdom of this world stems from our fear. This acknowledgment will initiate the reconnection process that allows us to uncover divine mysteries that surpass language and fear.

Given our deep immersion in worldly wisdom, many struggle to find genuine answers regarding our origins and existence. Consequently, many turn to the Bible, which serves as an excellent starting point for that exploration.

However, to truly understand our spiritual nature we must transcend traditional clichés in our interpretations of the scriptures, particularly in the book of Genesis. This book is significant as it unveils the intangible essence of God in a manner that can be perceived.

Moses wrote the Book of Genesis after spending 80 days with God without food or water. This profound experience allowed him to use divine language to describe creation.

After creating man and assigning him the task of naming all the animals, God divided him and took away his feminine side to serve as his companion. Shortly after this separation, God made it clear that eating from the forbidden tree would lead to death.

> *"except the tree that gives knowledge of what is good and what is bad. You must not eat the fruit of that tree; if you do, **you will die the same day**."*
>
> Genesis 2:17 TEV

The fact that man did not physically die demonstrates that God's Word is spiritual. He was referring to man's loss of spiritual authority and access to God's kingdom.

Adam was a spiritual entity in physical form, which granted him mastery over this physical realm until he made a poor choice. He chose the wisdom from this dimension, which has become the default condition for all beings born into this realm. Furthermore, we are all taught to rely on our five senses to define reality. Thus, we create our world based on this condition and believe it to be real.

This way of thinking encourages a problem-solving approach focused on the material world as the source of our troubles. In simple terms, we often perceive our challenges solely as results of physical situations, which obscures our understanding of our nature as spiritual beings.

Losing our spiritual connection with God makes it nearly impossible to perceive or comprehend a reality beyond this dimension. This results in a sense of separation from wholeness, instilling fear and driving us to seek security in material possessions.

The result of man losing his original design as spirit forced him to use his senses to create a picture that his body and brain rely on to protect an image. Recognizing this is crucial for understanding our origin and purpose.

The woman's quest for wisdom drove her to taste the forbidden fruit. This belief persists in this system, nurturing generations who believe that God thinks like they do, so their thoughts are His thoughts. Our perception shapes our reality, guided by the wisdom we embrace and communicate.

Our mental concepts and conditions are shaped by the sin consciousness of Adam, which is why Jesus clearly articulated His origin.

> *Jesus answered, "My kingdom doesn't belong to this world. If My kingdom belonged to this world, My followers would fight to keep Me from being handed over to the Jews. **My kingdom doesn't have its origin on earth.**"*
>
> John 18:36 GWT

Adam recalled that after consuming the fruit, God declared that death would be the result of partaking of the forbidden tree, an assertion that instilled fear in him. Thus, "fear" serves as the foundation inside all matter within this dimension.

Before eating the fruit, Adam named all the creatures on the earth and communicated with God. It was not until fear entered his being that he lost his spiritual bandwidth to God's kingdom, which connected him with the divine and the mysteries of the universe. This perfectly illustrates why Jesus said to make that discovery our top priority.

The fear of death serves as the fundamental frequency for all matter in this dimension. It flows through the blood, guiding entities to reproduce specific patterns. This is why offspring exhibit similar features and habits.

In other words, diseases attributed to genetics result from family beliefs and fears that are transmitted through the bloodlines of their offspring. I contend that this phenomenon is an outcome of the spiritual ailment, which we all inherit at birth, referred to as sin consciousness.

On the other hand, genes act like a personal fingerprint; they are not a foolproof way to predict conditions and diseases in families. The varying outcomes seen in identical twins illustrate this point. One twin may be diagnosed with a disease that their sibling never has.

If civilizations integrated this truth into their education systems, we could cultivate more profound awareness and create a more conscious generation from the very beginning. Even though humanity is born disconnected from God because of the sin consciousness of Adam, understanding our origins could guide individuals to the teachings of Christ more swiftly than in past generations.

The transformation in our lives will accelerate in ways we cannot even imagine when we trust our original design as spirit. Embracing this simple truth invites the guidance of the Holy Spirit into our daily lives, as it seamlessly shifts our perceptions from the material to the spiritual.

As spiritual beings, we intuitively understand the truth, which is why we follow Christ's teachings. This practice allows us to align with frequencies that silence the voices of doubt and disbelief, which can flood our minds with fear.

Do you recall the thrill of purchasing a new car and suddenly noticing its make and model everywhere? This vividly demonstrates how the Holy Spirit shifts our perception and understanding, allowing us to see what has always existed within our spirit.

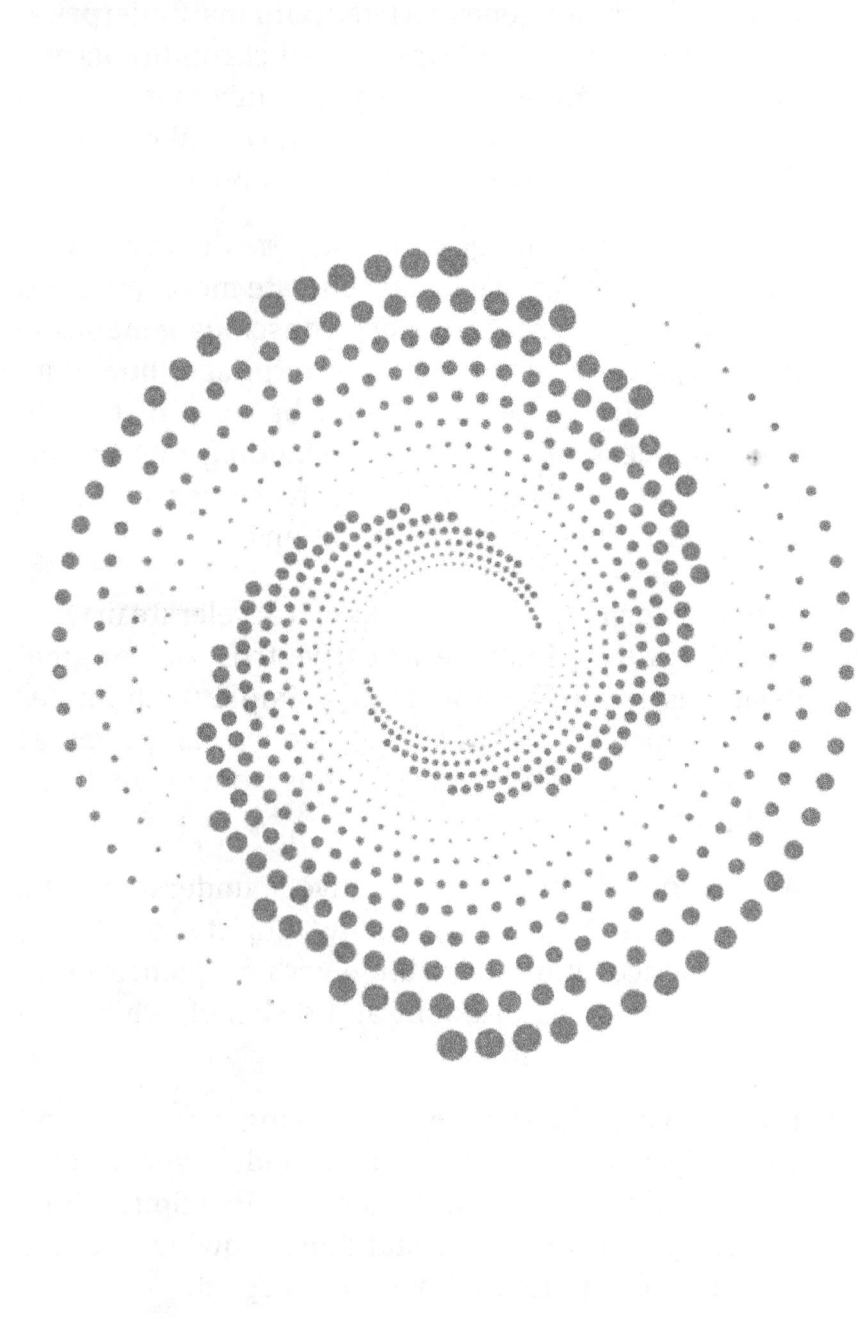

BETWEEN
DIMENSIONS

Those devoted to their relationship with their Creator will joyfully celebrate the remarkable journey we share and will wholeheartedly trust in the wonderful process that His love has designed to lead us back to Him.

We realize that our origin goes beyond just our physical birthdays; it comes from the nonlinear dimension beyond time. Embracing this idea can inspire us to rethink what truly matters to us in life.

Nevertheless, it remains our responsibility to observe our current condition to receive instructions from the Holy Spirit to facilitate our position IN HIM.

> *Praise the God and Father of our Lord Jesus Christ! Through Christ, God has blessed us with every spiritual blessing that heaven has to offer.*
>
> *Before the creation of the world, He chose us through Christ to be holy and perfect in His presence.*
>
> Ephesians 1:3-4 GWT

Paul provided an insight into our origins and, dare I say, our current state. I invite you to reflect with me for a moment. If we existed prior to the establishment of a "world," which, as we have learned, is a product of our belief, it stands to reason that altering our belief would consequently change our position.

I understand the effort we've all put into shaping our image and navigating our circumstances, which can make it challenging to leap into the unknown. Still, we are here to carry out the important assignment that He entrusted to us even before we took on flesh.

Moreover, it's essential to recognize that our time in this dimension is finite, offering us a brief opportunity to explore the mysteries that Jesus revealed to His disciples after His resurrection. These insights are bestowed upon anyone who sincerely follows Jesus' teachings in pursuit of His Kingdom. Believe me, they are crucial keys that will unlock visions, dreams, and revelations not accessible through any other means.

■ IMAGELESS TRANSFORMATION

I awoke one morning to a vision of myself suspended by what appeared to be strings. This image resembled a puppet controlled by a hand detached from a body; however, as it moved, so did my image. It felt as though I was powerless to act except to move in the direction dictated by the hand manipulating the strings.

I perceived the Holy Spirit guiding me to remain mindful of both the image and the hand. Immediately, my perspective shifted from a three-dimensional viewpoint to a multidimensional space. I knew this because I could not identify anything with my senses. In the third dimension, objects are defined by shadows and light, as well as our cognitive recognition of shapes and sizes.

Therefore, beyond this dimension, it becomes difficult to discern or even locate objects, which led me to cease searching for the familiar and allow the Holy Spirit to impart what He wanted me to understand without my attempting to distinguish the object.

In that moment, it became clear to me that what I was experiencing was my origin beyond the limits of time and space. I felt a deep sense of knowing and understanding arising simultaneously within me. There was no usual search for cause and effect that I often engage in within this dimension. Instead, it was an innate understanding, a knowing that transcended traditional teaching, and that's what truly shapes my perception of the invisible realm.

As I stayed calm and aware, the movements around me began to slow down, and suddenly, the light felt like it paused in time. In that peaceful moment, my mind started to wander, and I found it a bit challenging to maintain my focus with all the random distractions trying to pull me away.

The energy it took for me to stay focused was constantly being depleted by wave after wave of thoughts and emotions. The random thoughts flashing through my mind were vibrating at such a low frequency that I became exhausted. Nevertheless, the longer I attempted to remain conscious, the stronger I became until at once the battle ended.

In that moment, I clearly heard the Holy Spirit gently remind me that the struggle to remain present in this world is, in fact, the most important battle we must confront to break free from our conditioning.

Each day, we find ourselves in a dilemma of dimensions, grappling with thoughts that try to convince us we're separate from our challenges. The reality is, we mirror what we resist. Additionally, the more we justify our position, the more energy we use that could help us stay anchored in the present.

For instance, during my childhood, I played baseball and was always competing for a place on the team. Many of my teammates were just as skilled, if not more so, than I was, so I needed to find ways to stand out to secure my spot. I recall perceiving my rivals as enemies, which led me to rationalize fabricating lies and spreading rumors about them to boost my image in the coaches' eyes. In reality, the majority of the falsehoods I ascribed to my competitors reflected my own traits and weaknesses.

Identifying differences in others separates us from God's Oneness and the Holy Spirit's guidance. I learned that viewing competition as part of myself ensures I cannot fail, as Oneness guarantees everyone's success through Christ's victory over separation.

Our attachment to images and emotions shapes our physical state and ultimately forms the image we protect and validate. It's essential to recognize that our observations of circumstances are neither good nor bad until we choose to judge them.

Judgment is what separates us from our heavenly position and establishes us as an image we passionately defend and validate. This marks the beginning of turmoil and tribulation until we consciously acknowledge these phenomena as they occur.

Moving through this dimension as physical beings conditioned by our experiences involves numerous opinions about right, wrong, good, and bad. It's not our opinions that create division among us; instead, it's the belief that we hold some sort of superiority over an image that we've unknowingly helped bring to life.

In simpler terms, since we shape the world around us, it means that the characters in this melodrama stem from our own imaginations.

Engaging in that practice is a fool's errand that distracts us from the divine present moment, which was shaped by the mind of Christ to transform our thinking and condition and seat us in the heavenly dimensions.

As we consistently observe our thoughts without judgment and let go of ideas that tie us to our understanding of reality, waves of joy will start to envelop us, transforming our perceptions and thoughts. The longer you remain in that state the more you will remember about your origin. This exercise fuels my daily struggle, particularly concerning my attitudes and reactions in this physical realm.

I have been amazed by the speed at which my perception has changed. I attribute this directly to the Spirit increasing my frequency to see the unseen realm. Everything I discover has always been there but hidden from me due to my bandwidth. These are terms that describe our magnetic self, which is the invisible being hidden inside our flesh bodies.

> *"Dismiss your fears, little flock: your Father finds a pleasure in giving you the Kingdom."*
>
> Luke 12:32 WEY

That scripture was just a concept for me until I practiced staying conscious each day. That habit enabled me to resonate with divine frequencies that opened my spiritual eyes to see and understand that His magnificent kingdom dwelt within me.

Choosing not to react to people or events, even when our analytical mind finds a reason to do so, opens heaven for us to move between dimensions and observe vibrations and light in entirely new ways. It was this light that allowed me to see the hand holding the strings.

I initially thought Jesus was the being of light holding the strings, but I soon realized it was me. This revelation changed me forever; I became certain that no unseen hand controlled my life. I was the creator of my life.

In other words, my conditioned beliefs were the strings moving the puppet and not the hand.

This vision broadened my understanding. My initial helplessness scared me until I realized fear alerts me to my separation from Oneness. When I desire to experience something, I move away from my dimension of oneness in Him.

My awareness shifts from physical to spiritual each time I stop myself from dwelling on the past or future.

Therefore, my acceptance of responsibility as the unseen force within this dimension has shattered the illusion that I must rely on something or someone to transform me.

> *Jesus said to the Jews, "I can guarantee this truth: The Son cannot do anything on His own.* **He can do only what He sees the Father doing.** *Indeed, the Son does exactly what the Father does."*
>
> John 5:19 GWT

Jesus was truly experiencing His Father in the present moment, and I'm discovering that this is the only way we can truly remain in Him. The moment our minds drift to past or future thoughts, we lose that precious connection and waste valuable spiritual energy that we gather throughout our conscious experiences.

Once we truly believe we are In Him, our perceptions can soar beyond the limitations of this dimension. The more conscious I become, the less I crave experiences from the material world, making it easier to remain present.

It is important to recognize that for individuals relying on physical experiences to shape their identity and well-being, validating their challenges and hardships is an ongoing struggle. These difficulties stem from the physical conditioning we undergo during childhood, a topic that will be explored in a later chapter.

CHAPTER 2 BETWEEN DIMENSIONS

CHAPTER 3

HYPNOTIC PROGRAMMING

You are surely discovering things you already know and have been considering for some time, but God has you in a position now to go deeper than ever before into His marvelous ways.

This section provides insights into uncovering the treasures of our spirit. Our beliefs influence our experiences and often hinder our ability to awaken to the vibrant life around us. Unfortunately, many remain unaware of this due to subconscious conditioning from birth until about age six.

A newborn enters the world like a blank canvas, free from any memories or experiences imprinted in their mind.

Research indicates that a form of "hypnosis" occurs from birth to age six. During this period, a baby's brain grows rapidly, doubling in size within the first year and reaching 90% of an adult's brain size by age five.

During this developmental phase, our subconscious thoughts, behaviors, and perceptions become entrenched as habitual patterns we execute automatically every day. This phenomenon occurs due to the dormancy of the analytical or rational part of our brain, which processes and evaluates information. Lacking any filters or resistance, by the age of seven, individuals have assimilated a significant volume of data that greatly shapes their identity.

Please take a moment to reflect upon the following. We enter this physical realm devoid of memories and lacking language or communication tools. Remarkably, within the subsequent five years, we are molded to think and believe in ways that closely resemble those who provided for us.

Programming and conditioning occur when we enter a trance-like state as infants, akin to hypnosis. This explains our instinctual reactions to the environment at certain moments.

I can still picture stepping into that room and being hit by a wave of fear I couldn't quite understand. Over time, I discovered that when I was just seven years old, I had witnessed my brother being bitten by a dog in that very space. This memory brought forth that fear, because the feelings connected to that incident had conditioned my body and mind to react this way.

This illustrates a phenomenon called "conditioning". By observing our thoughts and reactions, we allow the Holy Spirit to access and erase our hypnotic conditioning. Additionally, it offers incredible insight into how to help others who are conditioned by fear.

Remaining present will enhance our understanding of how our mental and physical conditioning shapes our identities. This conditioning greatly influences analytical thinking, creating a "firewall" around our experiences to ensure we automatically react according to our programs.

Our beliefs stem from generational conditioning passed down by our ancestors. The so-called "truths" we hold were instilled in us by family and friends who were also conditioned by fear and unbelief.

▪ GENETICS AND BLOOD EMPHASIZED

Our generational beliefs are shaped by our direct connection to Adam's consciousness and lineage. This helps us understand why Jesus' blood comes from His Father and how His words spiritually resonate with us.

Humanity originated inside God, who is Spirit. A person's life force is the light of God, which manifests as blood to sustain physical life on this planet. When God breathed into Adam's nostrils, he became a living soul.

Adam's unbelief introduced death into the heart and soul of all mankind born in this three-dimensional realm. Unbelief, or sin, corrupted humanity's life force, represented by blood, although it was originally the light of the first day.

A significant number of individuals and scientists mistakenly believe that genetics governs our physical state. This viewpoint fosters a victim mentality, leading to the erroneous belief that external assistance is necessary for their well-being. This should explain humanity's default condition to "run" to a doctor to receive relief from discomfort and pain.

Science often dismisses God as the Creator of all things, which unfortunately negatively influences many aspects of society. However, if science were truly omnipotent, the physical and mental conditions around the globe would reflect a much healthier situation.

God made us creators; viewing ourselves as victims creates a self-fulfilling prophecy. Why does this occur? As creators, we possess the power to shape our world and experiences. This understanding will become clearer as you read on.

In the presence of God, unexpected occurrences are nonexistent, as the solution was determined long before humanity disobeyed God. The key to understanding this magnificent plan, and its unfolding, lies in the teachings of Christ.

CHAPTER 3 ❙ HYPNOTIC PROGRAMMING

> *"I have told you this so that you might have peace in **Me**. In the world you will have trouble, but take courage, **I have conquered the world**."*
>
> John 16:33 NKJ

The Earth remains and will perpetually be God's heaven within this dimension. As creators, we manifest the world that we have been conditioned to believe exists. Remember that the terms "world" and "Earth" are not the same.

However, the conditioning passed down through generations is shaped by fear and unbelief, distorting our perceptions and creating a reality that seems to reflect the tribulation described by Jesus.

Many Bible-believing, church-going individuals encounter challenges similar to those faced by those who do not attend church. Although they read and cite scriptures, they still wonder about what Jesus conquered as we continue to face difficulties. The answers to those questions and more are addressed in this book.

When we answer Jesus' call to seek His kingdom first, we gain clearer insights in all aspects of our lives. Those who undertake this remarkable journey often discover that their fears diminish, making them less likely to heed the wisdom of the world around them.

You may have encountered challenges that make you question the purpose of pursuing God's Kingdom. The key to answering that question—and many others—lies in observing our thoughts and actions. Taking this step allows the Holy Spirit to enter your life in a way you've never encountered before.

CHAPTER 3 — HYPNOTIC PROGRAMMING

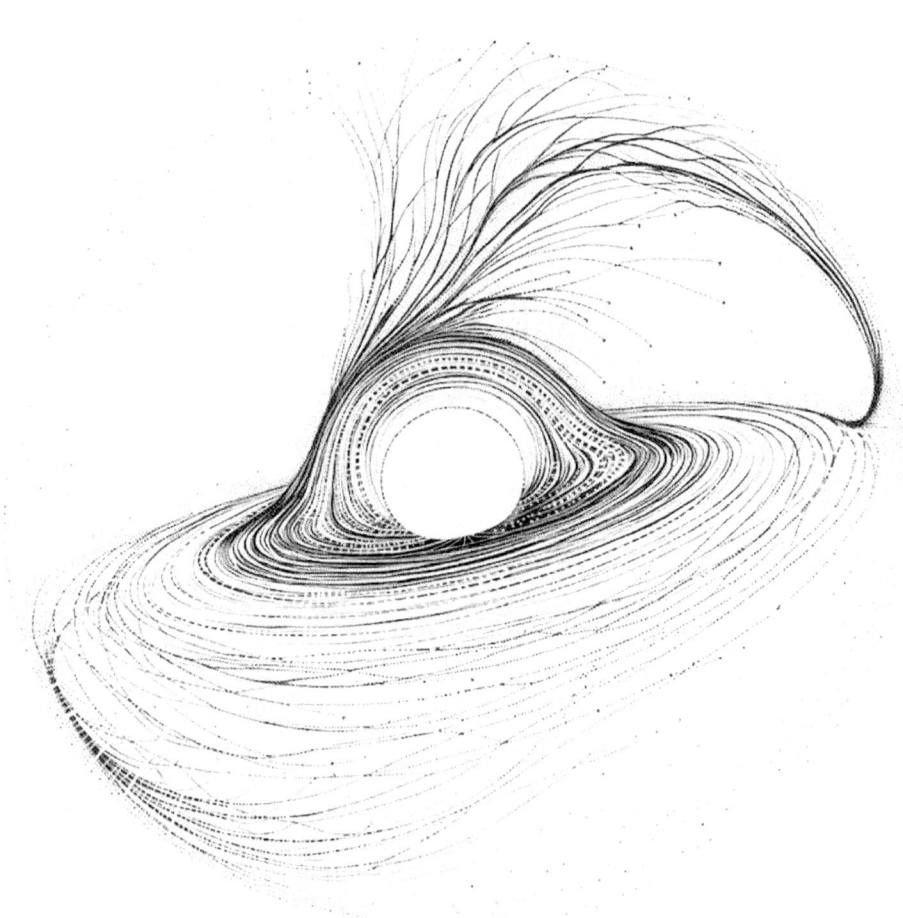

CHAPTER 4

SPIRITUALLY
PHYSICAL

Jesus' instructions located in the following verse must be our foremost priority; trust me, the process becomes increasingly effortless as your confidence grows with each moment you stay present.

> *"But seek first God's Kingdom, and His righteousness; and all these things will be given to you as well."*
>
> Matthew 6:33 WEB

This chapter will not only encourage us to reconnect with our origins but also provide tools. We will realize that what we have always sought to experience has always existed in the "eternal present" when viewed through the lens of rebirth. Why? Because we are in His kingdom as long as we remain in the eternal present moment.

Jesus' resurrection as the Christ was the most transformative event in human history. Although mankinds' physical world seemed unchanged, the heavens and earth experienced eternal transformation. The Kingdom of God reclaimed authority over the seen and unseen realms, while remaining invisible to those using their senses to navigate through life.

The power of that resurrection is accessible to anyone seeking the truth about our origins and purpose, but finding it demands a shift in perspective. Jesus called for repentance, yet many believe it simply means to cease committing the physical acts defined by the law of Moses in the Bible as sin.

We must reject the belief that anyone other than the Holy Spirit can truly interpret God's word. Jesus fulfilled the Old Covenant, and through His resurrection, He established a new covenant, enabling you to embody His living Word. This insight will show that those of us in covenant with the living Christ are the New Testament, not the books in the Bible following the page that proclaims "New Testament." This will become more than a concept once you study this book.

The desire to live spiritually, as the New Covenant requires, involves a new birth that transforms our trust from matter to spirit. This metamorphosis necessitates a conscious understanding that, as spirit, we must be guided by the Holy Spirit.

An important insight that has shaped my personal transformation is the careful study of Jesus' teachings. The following scriptures depict a conversation between Him and His Father, suggesting that, when understood through the lens of the eternal present, He continues to converse with His Son, who resides within those who have made a covenant with His resurrected self.

> *"I have not spoken on My own. Instead, the Father who sent Me told Me what I should say and how I should say it. I know that what He commands is eternal life. Whatever I say is what the Father told Me to say."*
>
> John 12:49-50 GWT

The scripture describes conversations with the Father in the past tense, but based on my experiences, that description is misleading. We are spirit, which is timeless, meaning words exist in the present, and the language created from this dimension does not adequately convey their intent or meaning.

The present moment transcends our current comprehension, which is constrained by the knowledge we have acquired within the boundaries set by the past and future. This is why Jesus emphasizes that His words are spirit.

The more we engage with the present, the fewer our thoughts wander to past concerns and future distractions. This realization nurtures mindfulness in the midst of chaos. I remember times when concentrating on the present allowed the Holy Spirit to unveil answers to questions I had posed years prior.

This moment sparked my transition from the physical world to the spiritual one, leading to an amazing encounter where I stood before a mirror that reflected nothing. In that moment, I heard His voice revealing that while the spirit has no physical form, it solves problems within our physical existence without requiring wisdom from this realm.

Adam was created in the way Jesus described as being "born again" to Nicodemus; however, as a spirit, he needed a physical body to govern the earth that he was destined to rule. In contrast, Jesus was born in the flesh, but there was a crucial difference. His incarnation allowed Him to inherit His Father's blood, which is passed on to everyone who is spiritually reborn through Him. Thus, the new birth He explained to Nicodemus requires all flesh to receive a divine transfusion of His blood.

At birth, we all share the condition of the fallen Adam, which is why God sent Jesus as the last Adam to illustrate the true essence of life as spiritually physical. In other words, Jesus was all flesh and all God, which is what it means to be spiritually physical.

His resurrection served as the ultimate evidence that He fulfilled all the prophecies about Him, despite the numerous interpretations of scripture that suggest a different scenario.

Additionally, He reinstated God's kingdom on earth in the forty days leading up to His ascension.

> until the day when He was taken up to heaven, after giving instructions through the Holy Spirit to the apostles whom He had chosen.
>
> **To these men He showed himself after His death and gave ample proof that He was alive: He was seen by them over a period of forty days** and spoke to them about the kingdom of God.
>
> Acts 1:2-3 REB

He moved among the disciples on Earth, often unnoticed, conveying messages through the Holy Spirit. Individuals who have been born again walk the Earth today, spiritually overlooked by those focused on the material world.

We often misinterpret scriptures due to our natural focus on the physical rather than the spiritual. Our familiarity with our physical state and senses causes us to make unconscious assumptions from that perspective, instead of relying on The Spirit to guide us back to our preexisting knowledge.

The treasure within us is more precious than anything in this dimension. We can tap into those gifts at will. However, our attention span is undisciplined; recognizing this is the first step toward unlocking our inner riches!

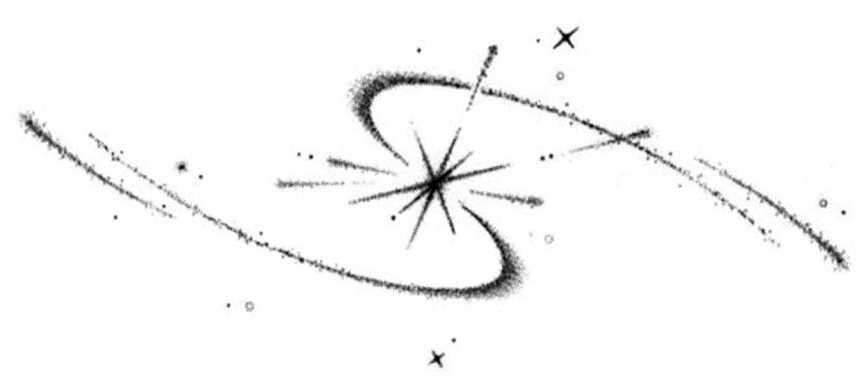

CHAPTER 5

DIVINE
TRANSFUSION

The only way to find God's kingdom is through the "new birth" described to Nicodemus. This chapter will provide keys that, when used with your current knowledge, will open your spiritual eyes to what has always existed.

The origin of all things earthly was heavenly, including God's idea for mankind. However, all creatures on Earth are born wearing their physical Earth suit, which is their birthright as citizens of this physical dimension.

God was not surprised by man's unbelief, as He always had a plan of redemption involving the ultimate sacrifice of Jesus.

He sacrificed His blood, acquired from outside this dimension, to atone for man's unbelief.

The divine transfusion was the hidden redemption that even satan did not know, or he would have never crucified Jesus.

The original design, before man's unbelief, was to transmit Adam's blood as God's son throughout all creation. Nevertheless, one of the functions of the Holy Spirit today is the preservation of humanity by maintaining the physical life force in the form of blood.

> *For there are three that bear testimony in heaven, **the Father, the Word, and the Holy Spirit**, and these three are one.*
>
> *And there are three that bear testimony on earth, the spirit, and the water, and the blood: and these three agree in one.*
>
> 1 John 5:7-8 NKJ

Jesus beautifully embodied the Father both as the Word and as Water, making His sacrifice a profound gift that offers humanity a chance for rebirth. The scriptures beautifully speak of the harmony in heaven and on earth as "testimony," which I interpret as being closely linked to covenant.

It's interesting to note that the Ark of the Covenant is also known as the Ark of the Testimony. God truly

CHAPTER 5 ❙ DIVINE TRANSFUSION

dwells within the covenants He establishes, and I believe the New Birth represents the very first step in forming our covenant with the resurrected Christ.

Water and blood are two of the most essential elements for our life on Earth, both of which originated from beyond this dimension within the Holy Spirit. This is why Jesus was sharing with Nicodemus that the concept of being reborn should be viewed from a heavenly perspective, encouraging us to repent.

> *Jesus answered him, "I assure you, most solemnly I tell you, that unless a person is born again (anew, from above), he cannot ever see (know, be acquainted with, and experience) the kingdom of God."*
>
> *Nicodemus said to Him, "How can a man be born when he is old? Can he enter his mother's womb again and be born?"*
>
> *Jesus answered, "I assure you, most solemnly I tell you, unless a man is born of water and [even] the Spirit, he cannot [ever] enter the kingdom of God.*
>
> *What is born of [from] the flesh is flesh [of the physical is physical]; and what is born of the Spirit is spirit."*
>
> John 3:3-6 AMP

Jesus imparts messages that resonate on a spiritual level, encouraging us to connect with the Spirit, who is the true source of illumination regarding His words. Although numerous churches strive to elucidate the concept of being born again through salvation, individuals who have undergone this experience understand that it encompasses far greater depth than merely that!

For instance, Jesus required a physical womb for His earthly birth. However, after His resurrection, He beautifully transformed into both God's kingdom and the spiritual womb through which we are baptized in water and Spirit. He embodied the fullness of this treasure by sharing that a "new birth" is essential for entry into the unseen realm of God's Kingdom.

This may seem impossible for the analytical mind, but that is why Jesus used the word repent, which means to change the way you think. This is why attempting to understand spiritual matters with a worldly mindset is futile. You can clearly see that in the following verses.

> *"The wind blows where it chooses, and you hear its sound, but you do not know where it comes from or where it is going. So is it with everyone who has been born of the Spirit."*
>
> *"How is all this possible?" asked Nicodemus.*

CHAPTER 5 | DIVINE TRANSFUSION

> *"If I have told you earthly things and none of you believe Me, how will you believe Me if I tell you of things in Heaven?"*
>
> John 3:8-9,12 WEY

To return to our origin and allow the Holy Spirit to reprogram our conditioned mentality, we must be "born again." This is not just a concept; it signifies the death of the programmed self-image shaped by our conditioning. The only way to overcome our condition mentally is through rebirth.

Jesus compares spiritual rebirth to the wind, emphasizing that just because something is invisible doesn't mean it lacks existence or power. This underscores the importance of exploring the mysteries and profound significance of His resurrection.

The resurrection of Christ has permanently transformed our existence, yet each person must discover that truth on their own. The lives we lead today reflect our beliefs, and these beliefs have repercussions in this world. This is why Jesus urged us to seek His kingdom, a place free from such consequences.

He is, was, and will eternally represent the essence of God's kingdom, which He proclaimed and mandated for all individuals to make priority as their physical life's objective.

Our emphasis on the physical after entering this realm is entirely natural. Nevertheless, we must remember our origins, as this is vital to experiencing the joy that God has graciously prepared for us from the start, as eloquently stated in Ephesians 1:4.

> *...even as, in His love,* **He chose us as His own in Christ before the creation of the world,** *that we might be holy and without blemish in His presence.*
>
> Ephesians 1:4

With infinite love, God offered salvation to everyone at the crucifixion; yet it was through His resurrection that we could reconnect with our spiritual essence, enabling us to experience this earthly life as spiritually physical.

Maintaining mindfulness of The Word gradually reshapes our thinking. The more we nurture this awareness over time, the more extraordinary our lives become. I will consistently emphasize this theme throughout this book, hoping that if you remember nothing else, this idea will resonate deeply in your subconscious.

Few words can adequately convey the profound peace within His kingdom, as there are no shadows that incite fear. Moreover, it is essential to keep in mind that one never fully arrives, because as you will comprehend, we never left our place in Him.

Begin where you are and mindfully notice the present moment, along with your thoughts. This practice enables the Holy Spirit to guide your focus toward the hidden truths that are right before you.

My principal objective throughout this book is to enhance the clarity of His voice to such an extent that it transcends into the very wind described by Jesus to Nicodemus.

Those wishing to explore the subject of new birth further can read my book entitled, *Immersed In Him*.

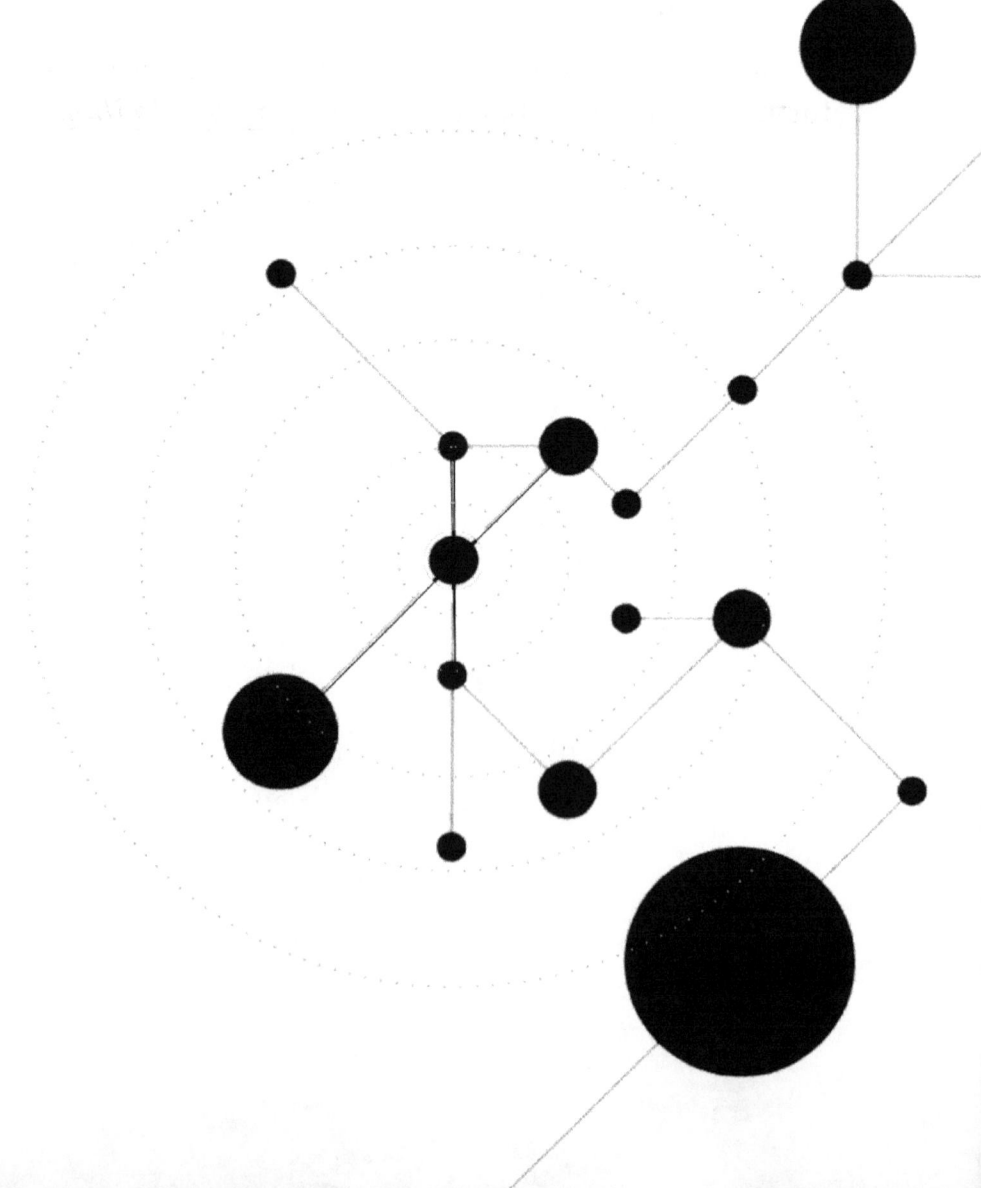

CHAPTER 6

WHAT DO YOU **BELIEVE** AND WHY?

If building contractors were to pinpoint the most important part of their structures, most would agree that it's the foundation. This principle holds true not just for buildings but also for our lives and the choices we make every day.

Everyone of us fortunate enough to have been raised by parents who loved one another and worshiped God has a distinct advantage in discovering God's love. Attending church is not the only way God reaches out, but it seems to be a common thread for many searching for answers to important questions, such as life's purpose.

The church provides a remarkable chance for individuals to encounter a love that goes beyond themselves, through Jesus. Yet, difficulties may emerge when people trained in this system try to interpret the Bible. Sadly, this can lead to a circumstance in which the impactful teachings of Christ lose their meaning and are obscured by worldly wisdom.

Through scripture and divine love, we discover a life beyond this world, sowing invisible seeds that flourish within us. These seeds often spark a longing to delve into life's profound mysteries, which are unattainable through religion, government, or success.

This longing truly encourages us to explore deeper meanings in the Bible, beyond the typical interpretations we frequently find in various churches or religious settings. I completely resonate with this feeling, and I wholeheartedly believe that the Holy Spirit often guides us in this direction.

The more we pursue our insatiable desire for answers to the profound questions about existence, the closer we come to the fire that ignites within each of us: the Holy Spirit. He alone can address these inquiries and clarify the teachings of Jesus.

> "However, the helper, the Holy Spirit, whom the Father will send in My name, will teach you everything. **He will remind you of everything that I have ever told you.**"
>
> John 14:26 GWT

The Holy Spirit began teaching me the Bible from within, differing from traditional reading methods. Our world operates in a linear fashion, with beginnings and endings, right and wrong, good and bad. This linear motion, known as "duality", results from Adam's poor choice and underpins the wisdom and mentality of this dimension.

Yet, the spiritual realm transcends these boundaries, for eternity is simultaneously present and infinite. Additionally, written language has a restricted dimensionality until the Holy Spirit enhances it through our faith, revealing the multidimensional qualities of the spiritual realm.

You might recall that after Jesus' baptism, the Holy Spirit led Him into the wilderness. The purpose was to see if Jesus, born into a world ruled by satan, would fulfill His mission or succumb to temptation, much like Adam did. Naturally, He passed this trial successfully and then began searching for His disciples.

The term "disciple" is derived from "discipline," highlighting our individual training to recognize the Spirit. In my case, fasting was part of my preparation, yet the Spirit uses diverse methods to achieve outcomes that are impossible through any other means. Without discipline, the mysteries of Christ stay hidden, as noted in the following verse:

> **And the disciples** came and said to Him, "Why do you say things to them in the form of stories?"

> *And He said to them in answer, **"To you is given the knowledge of the secrets** of the kingdom of heaven, but to them it is not given."*
>
> Matthew 13:10-11 BBE

Count yourself blessed if He has enlisted you in His discipleship program. Your life will never be the same again. The Bible will open like a scroll to reveal hidden treasures never before seen, propelling you beyond your *image* and *conditioning*.

First, you'll learn that much of what we were taught from the Bible is false or only partially true. Secondly, and most crucially, you'll discover we are not merely reflections in a mirror. This image creates a persona that reinforces our misguided faith in the physical realm, which is why Jesus states the following:

> **" Life is spiritual.** Your physical existence doesn't contribute to that life. The words that I have spoken to you are spiritual. They are life."
>
> John 6:63 GWT

> "It is the Spirit Who gives life the flesh conveys no benefit whatever [there is no profit in it]. **The words** (truths) that I have been speaking to you are spirit and life."
>
> John 6:63 AMP

The scripture in John holds deep significance. The words and teachings of Christ resonate at a frequency beyond this physical dimension, encapsulating both life and spirit. Life transcends mere existence, encompassing more than just a heartbeat or physical form.

When our physical state resonates with Christ's words, our understanding transforms. The present moment serves as the best access point to engage with that vibrational frequency. Our origin is rooted in this vibration, along with all visible things.

> *He is before all things, and in Him all things hold together.*
>
> Colossians 1:17 NAB

The previous verse shows that God is not contained by eternity; instead, eternity exists within Him. By deepening our understanding, we can recall our position in Him, as indicated in the next verse.

> *according as **He did choose us in Him** before the foundation of the world, for our being holy and unblemished before Him, in love,*
>
> Ephesians 1:4 YLT

This verse indicates that we existed in Him before the *foundation of the world*. To grasp this, we must embody His Word, which necessitates remembering that outside this dimension, language is light without shadows.

This may sound strange until you realize Spirit is God and God is light. This is not merely a concept or a cliché; it encapsulates our present identity and our origin.

A. BRAIN AND BODY

As we investigate the roots of our beliefs, we quickly realize that we often lack clarity on how many of our views and opinions were formed. Reflecting on this serves as a significant first step and should be a daily practice.

Even if the reasons for our beliefs are unclear, we need not panic. A lack of a definitive answer is preferable to a knee-jerk reaction to a program. The first step in unlearning our automatic responses is to remain aware in the present moment. It may sometimes feel like you are in a void, but this is actually a valuable space to explore.

When the body aligns with the brain—guided by the spirit—an elegant balance is achieved. The challenge arises from the tendency of most people to be led not by the spirit but by their memories and emotions. For many, the primary goal is to attain predictability and comfort, which prevents the Holy Spirit from guiding us to where He desires.

The brain serves as the body's primary processing unit (CPU), similar to an unprogrammed hard drive until it is shaped by the frequencies and vibrations of its environment. This remarkable organ can store memories, release neurotransmitters, and perform creative tasks at impressive speeds. Moreover, it forms a network of both short-term and long-term memories, constructed from the emotions linked to those experiences. Essentially, the memories that affect the body most profoundly are those associated with the greatest pain.

The hypothalamus is an organ that produces essential chemicals in the human body to correspond with our feelings and emotions. For instance, when a person experiences injury, sadness, depression, or elation, the body sends a signal to the brain, prompting it to release the necessary chemical compounds that align with the corresponding emotional state.

The upcoming sections and chapters will deepen our understanding of the layers of deception that have instilled fear and led to corrupted choices, the consequences of which inflict pain and suffering on those who cherish the Lord.

B. EMOTIONAL ADDICTS

Over the past five decades, the planet's population has developed an addiction to feelings, regardless of their long-term detrimental effects on the body's organs.

This pursuit has compromised both the physical and psychological balance of the population, leading to conditions that only the Holy Spirit can resolve.

The addiction to emotions such as sadness, depression, anxiety, victimization, insecurity, jealousy, and bitterness, among others, has severely impaired the body's capacity to adequately produce the chemical compounds necessary to meet the body's requirements.

Consequently, science has invested billions in corporations and pharmaceutical companies to ensure that people are medicated from birth, which ultimately creates lifelong dependencies and adversely affects immune systems. For instance, newborns are required to receive vaccinations at birth, like the Hepatitis B vaccine, which is designed for those at risk due to unprotected sexual activity.

Mandating this vaccine for infants linked to liver disease is unreasonable and should be discontinued. Often, the result is that many infants become reliant on one of the several medications associated with the vaccines, effectively turning them into lifelong legal drug addicts.

The consequences of a population dependent on medication are extensive and intricate. However, it is clear that fear fuels the reliance on synthetic drugs for immediate pain relief, potentially causing considerable long-term harm to several organs.

Financial gain motivates drug production; if humanity embraced the resurrected Christ and abandoned fear, pharmaceutical companies would close. The result would be dramatic in the future generations.

Consider this: the body, created by God, is hijacked by the promise of pain relief through synthetic chemicals that ultimately enslave you. The lies we believe come from our conditioning and emphasis on flesh over spirit.

Interestingly, individuals can experience emotions physically, even in the absence of external triggers. This indicates that irrational fears associated with past traumas remain as memories. When we cling to these emotions, it complicates our ability to concentrate on anything beyond the tangible world.

The beautiful connection between the brain, mind, matter, and spirit is deeply interwoven, as God created everything from within Himself, which is spirit. **This is why it's so important for us to focus on wholeness and understand that separation is merely a product of this world's system designed to control the population through fear.**

All forms of energy communicate their presence through frequency, eliminating the need for gazelles to determine whether a lion is an adversary or ally. They instinctively sense the lion's nature through its vibrational frequency, which serves as the nonverbal communication mechanism inherent to all of God's creation. Every entity within God's creation oscillates both within and beyond this dimension.

All matter consists of atoms that function as energy waves until you, as a conscious observer, convert the unknown into a concrete image, a phenomenon we refer to as "the collapse of a wave". These waves remain interconnected with God. This connection serves as our source and refuge unless we choose to separate ourselves from this state by focusing on past events or pondering the future.

As creators, we have the freedom to think and believe as we choose. This empowers many individuals to harness their will and creativity to create a world filled with characters that evoke emotions and drama. Recognizing this role is one of the benefits of remaining present.

Remember, nothing is inherently good or bad until we make a choice. However, if we believe in our imagination, we will embody a character in the world we create. This process typically begins with a desire to experience something that fosters singularity rather than oneness.

Many doctor visits arise from perceived ailments fueled by fear, leading patients to accept diagnoses from a profession that emphasizes the language of death, as its business model thrives on illness rather than health.

Doctors and scientists frequently perceive the body as a machine comprised of different parts. This viewpoint limits their comprehension of the body as a cohesive organism and overlooks the effects of fear and imagination. Consequently, it results in a symptom-centered treatment approach that relies on medications, which can ultimately harm the body.

Every illness is named, encouraging pharmaceutical companies to collaborate with drug manufacturers on media campaigns that promote their products. As a result, television viewers frequently relate to the symptoms showcased, prompting them to consult with their local physician.

Illness, like all physical phenomena, exists within a conscious being before it becomes apparent in this realm. Quantum science reveals that all possible existences are already present, but they become actualized when a conscious observer interacts with a thought or image. A disease often emerges when a conscious being thinks about or frequently mentions the name diagnosed by the doctor for the illness.

Individuals who embrace consciousness fully inhabit the vibrant present moment, and are blessed with incredible spiritual gifts. This wonderful state empowers people to transcend fear, fostering a deep trust that God has already provided for all their needs. This truly offers just a glimpse into the remarkable power that God has generously bestowed upon those who choose to be fearless.

From my experience, accepting responsibility for my circumstances allows the Holy Spirit to unveil the resurrected Christ, elevating me beyond my perceived state and situation. Sadly, many individuals see themselves as victims, strengthening and validating their current condition.

C. THOUGHTS AND MIND

> *After all, who knows everything about a person except that person's own spirit? In the same way, no one has known everything about God except God's Spirit.*
>
> *Now, we didn't receive the spirit that belongs to the world. Instead, we received the Spirit who comes from God so that we could know the things which God has freely given us.*
>
> *We don't speak about these things using teachings that are based on intellectual arguments like people do. Instead, we use the Spirit's teachings. We explain spiritual things to those who have the Spirit.*
>
> 1 Corinthians 2:11-13 GWT

One of Paul's most significant letters to the Corinthians, who were heavily influenced by Greek philosophy, remains relevant today. It teaches us that our conditioning and mindset often serve as the greatest obstacles to understanding the truth.

This section serves as a guide to help you stay focused and aware of your condition. Understanding your true essence as a spirit will ultimately equip you with the necessary tools for life, while empowering the Holy Spirit to order your steps.

Therefore, please refer to this section more frequently as your attention span increases because what you read now will expand your bandwidth or perception as your attention increases.

We have discovered that our thoughts carry spiritual energy that will transform atoms into our beliefs. The speed of this transition depends on our spiritual unity.

In other words, if our mind and heart are in unison with the idea or thought the manifestation is visible, regardless of what our senses may report. Why? Because outside this time/space realm everything already is.

Thought demands energy and focus, moving atoms and generating vibrations. Our reliance on predictability—food, people, and events—reinforces daily patterns, making life predictable. This pattern arises from fear, hindering the Holy Spirit's guidance.

This forms an environment or bandwidth that provides security for our bodies and brains, causing our thoughts to remain anchored in the

past or future. The fear of death is the most effective stimuli needed for programming behavior on this planet.

We learn to be afraid as part of our conditioning, which requires us to learn what choices to make that will protect us from situations we cannot control or predict.

This conditioning initiates a cycle of making the same choices, generating the same feelings and producing the same experiences, ultimately reproducing the same behavior.

Science reports that we generate about 70,000 thoughts daily, with 90% being identical. This results in the same experiences and outcomes as the previous day, creating an endless cycle of programmed choices.

This is why we can generate the same feelings in our minds without any external influence. This is also why people experience panic attacks and other ailments without any outside triggers instigating the condition.

From birth, the unconscious conditioning we experience profoundly influences the self-image we see in the mirror. This relationship with our self-image fosters a core belief that can serve as a comforting blanket, softly lulling many into a dreamlike state as they journey through life.

The mind is spiritual and designed for connection with God, but achieving this connection requires remaining present, consuming a great deal of energy. However, cultivating awareness actually conserves energy, allowing for longer periods spent in the spiritual realm while operating within this dimension.

> *For who has knowledge of the mind of the Lord, so as to be His teacher? But we have the mind of Christ.*
>
> <u>1 Corinthians 2:16 BBE</u>

The present moment is genuinely eternal and nonlinear, offering us the joy of experiencing multiple dimensions. One of the initial signs that we've deviated from this beautiful state is when thoughts from the past or future start to intrude upon us. When this occurs, simply observe this phenomenon without judgment. Breathing stabilizes our nervous system and induces calm. Resisting fear aids us in finding inner stillness.

Thoughts exist as both waves and particles, taking on an elliptical form when experienced in the moment. By consistently focusing on the present, we enhance frequencies, transforming wavelength patterns into spiral shapes. This change modifies our bandwidth and sharpens our perception. These states transcend the limits of time, often overlooked by those focused on material concerns or physical sensations. This practice is essential if you want to change your perception and elevate your awareness.

Thoughts of the past and future create wave patterns that keep us entranced by feelings like lack, pain, or desire. This is evident when someone drives for hours, only to realize they were unaware of their journey.

In other words, the brain often controls our attention, but recognizing this struggle makes us wiser and more resilient against distractions. Over time, your awareness will grow as you become increasingly mindful of the brain's tendency to divert your focus with distracting fears from the past.

The invisible realm uncovers the truth of this dimension, showing that what we see are shadows without substance. The mindset shaped by our interaction with eternity enhances our perception and attention span beyond the physical world. You must explore this yourself to truly experience your rightful place in the heavenly realms.

The mind of Christ generates thoughts that resonate at frequencies beyond this dimension, which are eternal. As we gain a deeper understanding of the unseen realm, we find ourselves less swayed by the illusions we previously accepted as reality. This enables us to interpret scripture in a way that markedly differs from previous teachings.

Remember, you are a spirit! Feel inspired! Your journey has no limit. Deep down, we've always known this truth but may not have fully embraced it until now. Now, we have both the capacity and desire to enjoy each moment!

CHAPTER 6 — WHAT DO YOU BELIEVE AND WHY?

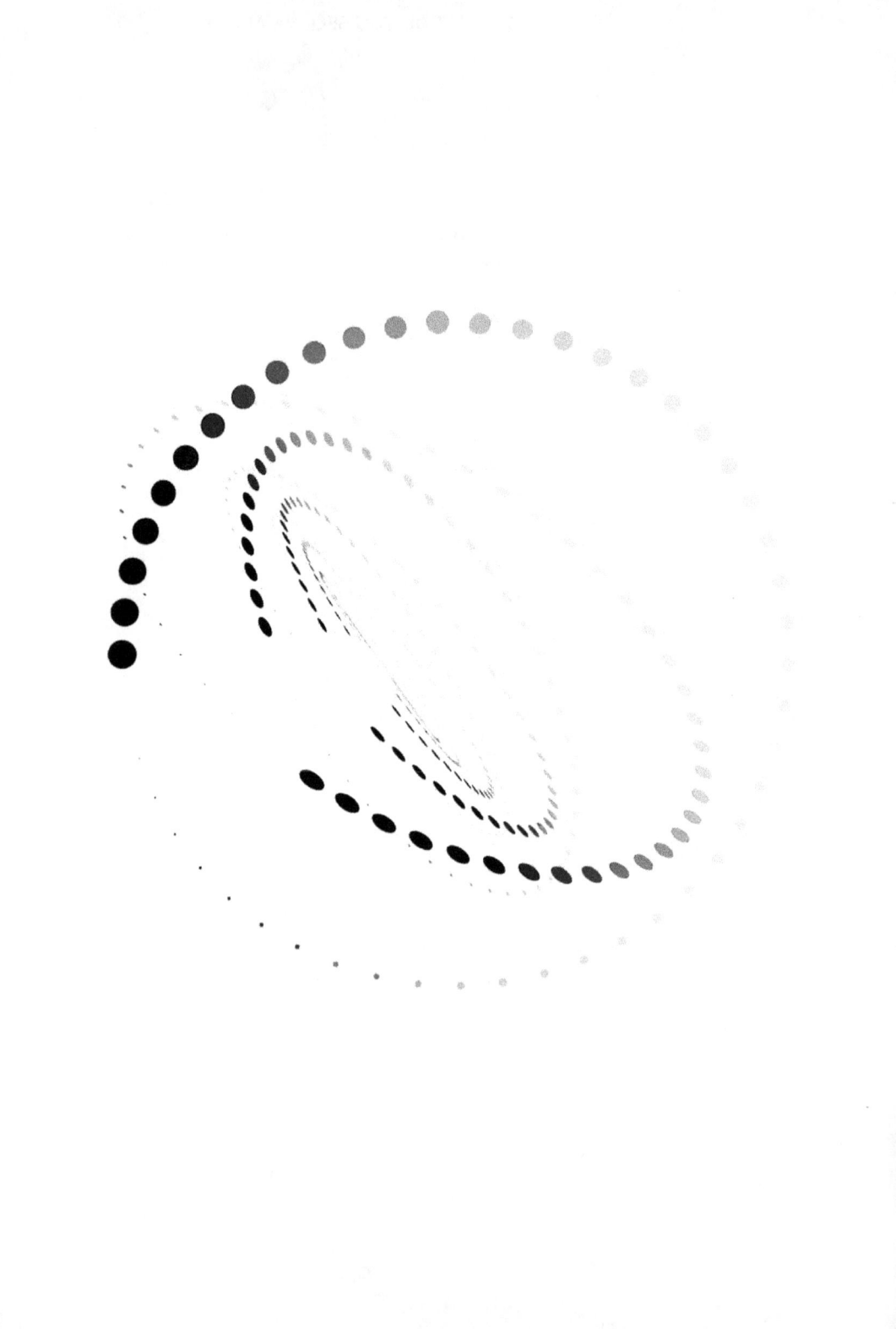

CHAPTER 7

MONEY AND **IMAGINATION**

This section highlights imagination as the driving force behind our belief in the illusions of money as the primary means of validating our separation within this dimension. For instance, individuals from all walks of life, including religion, politics, education, and family, invest significant time and energy in the concept of money. What accounts for this?

This dimension is material, so there must be a means to acquire matter known as money. Yet, currency lacks life or death, and it doesn't hold a soul or spirit. As the verse below shows, this doesn't stop people from loving it.

> *for a root of all the evils is the love of money,*
>
> 1 Timothy 6:10(a)

Human beings are conditioned to believe that money gives the freedom to choose a belief reflecting our faith in fairy tales, which stems from our fear of death.

Some religious groups associate prosperity, often seen as material wealth, with faith. They cite a verse from Paul in Galatians 6:7, which says, *"For whatever a man sows, that he will also reap."* This scripture holds true due to the laws operating within this limited dimension of duality. Additionally, it clarifies why God established the Law temporarily in this realm and explains the physical manifestation of our thoughts and beliefs.

This principle underpins classical physics, as we discussed. However, true kingdom prosperity is outlined by Jesus in Matthew. Therefore, if we want to live "spiritually physical" lives like Jesus, we must genuinely understand the following verse:

> *"Look at the birds which fly in the air: they do not sow or reap or store up in barns, but your Heavenly Father feeds them: are not you of much greater value than they?"*
>
> Matthew 6:26 WEY

Jesus represents prosperity in His kingdom, while Paul outlines the principles of the worldly system defined by the law that Jesus fulfilled. Those in a covenant with Jesus frequently find themselves operating under the law, which can lead to a love of money.

This happens because many churches focus on law-based messages that highlight prosperity through sowing and reaping. Such teachings subtly keep individuals ensnared within this worldly system.

But Christ and His kingdom are now the ruling kingdom, and as He said, *"it is His pleasure to give us that kingdom."* I choose to believe Him and operate with that belief, battling thoughts and imaginations that suggest that I need money for happiness, security and prosperity.

Staying focused in the moment negates thoughts of lack. Why? The physical realm operates slower than the spiritual, highlighting that fear—our source of anxiety and separation—is an illusion.

So, our source of provision is designed to be in harmony with our awareness. When we realize that we've always had what we need, it lessens the impulse to confirm this truth by looking at our bank balance. The more we embrace this mindset, the faster abundance appears in our lives.

Here is a technique that I have practiced that transforms my mentality. Abraham knew this principle, which is why he could see *the day of Jesus and be glad.*

> *"Your father Abraham rejoiced to see My day. He saw it, and was glad."*
>
> John 8:56 NKJ

The less we depend on fear-based beliefs, the more we can adopt a childlike perspective, particularly in imagination. For instance, children would straddle brooms as if they were riding horses. This playful innocence faded once we started school and learned to view adult behaviors as normal. The day we began to adopt that behavior we lost our innocence and ability to see God's kingdom. In fact Jesus said it most profoundly in the verse below:

> *"I can guarantee this truth: Whoever doesn't receive the kingdom of God as a little child receives it will never enter it."*
>
> Luke 18:17 GW

Abraham celebrated even before Jesus came to earth, as his childlike faith resonated with the reality of the spiritual realm that exists beyond time and space. This illustrates faith in action outside of time, where all possibilities are present.

Jesus had no attraction to this realm as His attention was focused on seeing and hearing the unseen realm. This verse beautifully illustrates that condition.

CHAPTER 7 — MONEY AND IMAGINATION

> *They brought a coin. He said to them, "Whose face and name is this?" They told Him, "The emperor's."*
>
> Mark 12:16 GWT

The scripture beautifully illustrates a mindset that thrives independently of this system as its source. Interestingly, Jesus was not even aware of what Caesar looked like, yet He offered His profound response grounded in principles of righteousness.

> *"Give to everyone who asks you for something, and when someone takes what is yours, do not ask for it back."*
>
> Luke 6:30 GWT

Moreover, how many people are ready to give without expecting anything in return? This reflects a disconnection so deep from the material world that it's evident why He could easily focus on the spiritual aspect.

If generating income is our objective, we must invest time and energy into this endeavor. This desire is reasonable, provided it doesn't take priority over finding God's kingdom. The main problem is that understanding this system requires embracing principles that sap the energy we need to remain present.

Jesus operated within the "order of Melchizedek" and demonstrated that we can have all our needs met in abundance while maintaining communication with the spiritual realm, which has always been the design.

If we see life as material rather than spiritual, we will channel our spiritual energy into that belief, becoming more material and less spiritual. Consequently, we may lose our ability to hear the Holy Spirit, who provides true solutions to our problems.

The fear of death serves as the fundamental principle in this world and is intricately linked to the doctrines of success. Essentially, those who attain success here bow to multiple fears and trust in the same wisdom that Adam relied on to reach their objectives. This subtly fosters a dependency on this world for their needs while dismissing what cannot be verified by their senses.

As those who were in Him before the world's foundation, we are called to embrace His completed work. Faith requires us to understand this truth beyond our sensory perceptions and to reject any contrary thoughts from our conditioned minds.

His death and resurrection reveal that all the experiences we seek already exist within us. Rather than pursuing these experiences externally, we need to acknowledge that they are already part of who we are. Our beliefs are the only barriers to accessing the treasures of this realization.

Resurrection transcends time and space, revealing my beginnings in Him. Imagination evolves into the certainty of what I comprehend. This is the outcome of resurrection.

My covenant with Christ provides me with His vision, beginning and concluding each day in resurrection over death. Every day starts and finishes with resurrection over death, illness, and disaster for everyone I know or will meet.

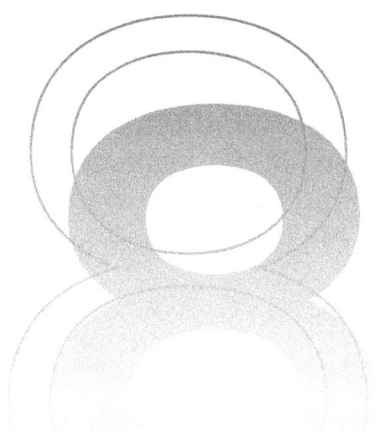

QUANTUM
SPEAK

Once you finish this section, you will recall your immense power and dismiss any thoughts of helplessness or victimhood. Furthermore, you will engage with the incredible mind of God, who has designed limitless dimensions for those brave enough to trust in the unseen.

For example, Jesus moved between visible and invisible realms with such grace that if you aren't paying attention, you might perceive Him as an ordinary man speaking normally. His words are spirit; each time we read them, we can transform into another dimension beyond our comfort zones.

The Book of Revelation illustrates John's effort to convey visions of the resurrected Christ. His covenant with Christ led him to experience revelations beyond what words in the Bible can express.

> *Then I saw another strong angel coming down from Heaven. He was robed in a cloud, and over his head was the rainbow. His face was like the sun, and his feet resembled pillars of fire.*
>
> *In his hand, he held a small scroll unrolled; and, planting his right foot on the sea and his left foot on the land,*
>
> *he cried out in a loud voice which resembled the roar of a lion. And when he had cried out, each of the seven peals of thunder uttered its own message.*
>
> Revelation 10:1-3 YNT

The face of the angel is the sun, or the first daylight in Genesis, or Jesus on the Mount of Transfiguration, which defines our origin and His voice as thunder, described several times in the scriptures when God spoke to His Son.

The angel referenced in the preceding verses represents Jesus, who fulfills the law and the prophets, signifying the end of the Old Testament.

CHAPTER 8 ▎ QUANTUM SPEAK

This all began with God's initial covenant, symbolized by the rainbow after the flood. This covenant, made with Noah and all living creatures on earth, signified that He would never again destroy His creation.

The angel stands on dry land and the sea, symbolizing the parting of the Red Sea during the Israelites' escape from Egypt. The scroll represents His law that saved Israel, and Jesus fulfilled it, thereby ending His covenant with Israel.

God fulfilled His covenants with His various servants, a topic to be elaborated upon in this book, to assure both you and me that we can individually enter into a covenant with Christ upon His resurrection.

Our personal covenant with the resurrected Christ is undoubtedly the most significant aspect of our lives. It not only serves as the primary purpose of this book but also provides solutions for any challenges you may encounter.

My quest to find a language that expresses our spiritual condition led me to explore quantum physics. However, I had no formal training in this field, resulting in my complete dependence on the Holy Spirit to connect the dots, as it were.

I found that replacing the word "spirit" with "energy" and "flesh" with "matter" provided me with a new perspective on rebirth. Although these verses may be familiar, their interpretation through a quantum lens has deepened my insights.

> *"What is born of flesh is flesh and what is **born of spirit is spirit.***
>
> ***Do not be amazed that I told you, You must be born from above.***
>
> ***The wind blows where it wills, and you can hear the sound it makes, but you do not know where it comes from or where it goes; so, it is with everyone who is born of the Spirit."***
>
> John 3:6-8 NAB

What Jesus spoke about was revealed to scientists nearly 2000 years later, as they discovered that all energy exists as both waves and particles. Quantum physicists demonstrated that energy remains in wave form until it becomes manifest in our dimension as matter, which represents the particle aspect of the wave.

Physicists call this process **collapsing a wave** and if you exchange the words energy and matter to spirit and flesh it provides a picture of being reborn in reverse.

Thus, the new birth is not truly a new birth in the spiritual realm because we are spirit. Therefore, instead of collapsing the wave, we return as the wave of the spirit back to our origin in Him.

This is why Jesus likened that transformation to the unseen wind. This illustrates why Jesus' words are considered spiritual—they originate from that realm—and why our spirit can discern the truth of that frequency.

> *"Life is spiritual. Your physical existence doesn't contribute to that life. The words that I have spoken to you are spiritual. They are life."*
>
> John 6:63 GWT

Governments are still spending billions of dollars in an attempt to understand what makes the unseen realm visible or what they term "collapsing the wave."

Unfortunately, the scientific community believes that reality exists only in this dimension, dismissing the spiritual. This viewpoint necessitates dependence on Newton's principles, the foundation of classical physics.

For example, Newton's first law of motion asserts that *"An object at rest remains at rest, and an object in motion continues in motion at a constant speed and in a straight line unless acted upon by an unbalanced force."*

Science uses mathematical principles to predict the behavior of all moving objects in this dimension. Matter follows these laws, shaped by the elements within the realm. Humanity applies these laws to structure their lives, as they offer predictability and a false sense of security against the unknown.

Subtly aligning with these laws, especially the first, makes us victims of circumstances. We become objects at rest, needing an external force to change our fate.

Classical physics has played a crucial role in contemporary developments in communication, travel, architecture, and overall comfort, offering reliable models that underpin our daily lives. Newtonian equations and laws originated from the observation of large objects, like the sun, moon, and planets, which displayed consistent behavior.

Physicists encountered challenges in their quest to understand the laws of unseen realms. This effort led to more questions than answers, ultimately directing scientists toward the field of quantum mechanics.

Quantum mechanics is the branch of physics that seeks to explain how very small entities, such as photons, atoms, and molecules, display properties of both particles and waves simultaneously. Physicists refer to this phenomenon as "wave-particle duality."

The "double-slit experiment" revolutionized physics by changing the emphasis from classical mechanics to quantum mechanics. Scientists found that traditional measurement methods could not provide reliable results because the observer's mental energy influenced the outcomes.

The term "observer effect" was coined to explain why predicting outcomes in quantum experiments is difficult. This insight shook the scientific community, as its credibility depends on predictable results.[1]

Quantum physics suggests that our awareness influences physical matter. This helps to clarify why Jesus spoke about dimensions beyond our own to exemplify faith and miracles.

> *as it is written, "I have made you father of many nations." He is our father in the sight of God, in whom he believed,* ***who gives life to the dead and calls into being what does not exist.***
>
> Romans 4:17 NKJ

The above scripture is describing the mentality of Abraham whose faith penetrated the invisible realm to manifest the unseen. This describes what physics refers to as "collapsing a wave".

Moreover, all life originates from the Spirit of God and requires atoms to exist in this dimension. Therefore, every person who has passed through this time-space continuum, including Jesus, interacted with the same atoms. This scripture in Colossians illustrates what science refuses to acknowledge:

> *For by Him all things were created that are in heaven and that are on earth, visible and invisible, whether thrones or*

---

[1] https://en.wikipedia.org/wiki/Observer_effect_(physics)

> *dominions or principalities or powers.* ***All things were created through Him and for Him.***
>
> Colossians 1:16 NKJ

Atoms, which are actually Christ, consist of energy waves made of invisible photons that engage with the mind of God to replicate according to His design and intention. What we refer to as solid matter is, in reality, empty space. Nevertheless, they exist as magnetic waves within this space-time continuum, suggesting they generate images based on the mental frequencies they encounter.

To put it another way, everything in creation reacts to fields of energy just like metal reacts to magnets. All the physical objects around us are actually images formed through our ability to recognize patterns. This means that what we perceive as solid objects are really waves of light that interact with our mind's energy to create the familiar patterns we know. In reality, we manifest what we identify and label as specific things.

You must understand this to detach yourself from whatever you believe is immovable.

Jesus famously stated that "a*ll things are possible with belief*," which acts as the spiritual force that changes energy into matter, a process that science refers to as "wave collapse".

This wave-collapsing process explains why Jesus expressed the thoughts He did in the following verse:

> *"Those who reject Me by not accepting what I say have a judge appointed for them. **The words that I have spoken will judge** them on the last day."*
>
> John 12:48 GWT

We understand that the words Jesus spoke are spirit, meaning they exist both within and beyond this time-space continuum, binding everything together and compelling all material things to adhere to their authority. They represent the energy that shapes all things, seen and unseen.

> *He existed before everything and holds everything together.*
>
> Colossians 1:17 GWT

If you reflect on the significance of His words, your physical connection to the visible world disappears like mist.

Newtonian models and equations rely on predictable factors, such as the speed of light, gravitational forces, and time, to yield quantifiable results.

Conversely, the quantum realm does not adhere to any of these forces, as the energy generated by the mind remains unquantifiable. Consequently, our thoughts represent the unknown variable that influences matter in unforeseen ways.

Time and light represent two fundamental elements of Earth that exert a profound influence on our perception and the material world. According to the biblical narrative, God created light on the first day, thereby establishing it as our primary source and origin, independent of time or shadows. Furthermore, it functions as the foundation for all life, as articulated in this following verse:

> **He was not the Light, but He existed that He might give testimony concerning the Light.**
>
> John 1:8

The illumination established on the fourth day was intentionally created in harmony with the universe to maintain the planet's balance within this dimension. It was not meant to distract humanity from relying on the light of the divine spirit that resides within each person.

Adam's regrettable choice resulted in humanity's reliance on their sensory perceptions, which are profoundly influenced by shadows and the passage of time.

> *And this is the test by which men are judged—the Light has come into the world, and men loved the darkness*

> *more than they loved the Light, because their deeds were wicked.*
>
> John 3:19 WEY

The light of Jesus dispels the darkness that people use to hide. Humanity fears death, and the light of Jesus terrifies those who have spent their lives believing the lies of darkness. Those who depend on the light of this world will always be frightened and hide from the truth.

As a result, when science develops tools to explain or uncover the unseen, such as in quantum studies, its conclusions are often flawed due to an understanding limited to this confined dimension. Solomon echoed this notion in Ecclesiastes 1:9, suggesting that nothing new can emerge from this realm.

Below are two translations of the same verse: one from Today's English Version and the other from God's Word Translation:

> *What has happened before will happen again. What has been done before will be done again.* **There is nothing new in the whole world.**
>
> Ecclesiastes 1:9 TEV

> *Whatever has happened before will happen again. Whatever has been*

> *done before will be done again. There is nothing* **new under the sun.**
>
> Ecclesiastes 1:9 GWT

Observe the connection between "world" and "sun." The sun, meant to govern this realm, was never intended to outshine those present in the first daylight. Nevertheless, people who rely on this dimension for answers will always repeat past mistakes.

I was taught that our spirit resides within us; in truth, we are spirit within "The Spirit". Without it, our existence would not be possible. It's crucial to understand that God is never separate from us; this separation occurs when we concentrate on matter instead of spirit.

> **For in Him we live and move and have our being,** *as even some of your own poets have said, 'For we are also His offspring.*
>
> Acts 17:28 NKJ

Jesus consistently illustrated the authority given to humanity; however, religion and misguided interpretations have robbed us of this knowledge. For instance, one of the most reliable factors in Newtonian physics is time, yet this does not apply in the quantum realm, where time is regarded as eternal.

In quantum physics, past, present, and future intricately intertwine. Time and matter are fundamentally relative in this dimension. If we see ourselves only as physical beings, our surroundings will reflect those beliefs.

Picture this: each morning, you rise with the inspiring belief that no obstacle can stand in your way as you shape a day filled with success. Yet, it's easy to let our conditioning and skepticism creep in, trying to shake this positive mindset by bringing up memories of past setbacks.

However, when we start focusing on the present moment, our memories lose their grip on our conditioned unbelief. Additionally, even if you face resistance, it can unveil opportunities you hadn't previously considered. I can't count how many times this has happened in my life.

The present moment is the kingdom of God, filled with every opportunity for our pleasure and enjoyment, because Jesus said it in the following verse:

> *"Do not be afraid any longer, little flock, for your Father is pleased to give you the kingdom."*
> Luke 12:32 NAB

Time demands matter conform to third-dimensional laws; all matter decays and ultimately returns to energy. This insight reveals a profound truth: all existence is inherently spiritual, governed by divine laws, not those discovered by humanity.

Even Einstein recognized God as the force transforming matter when he stated, *"The field is the sole governing agency on matter."* Unwittingly, Einstein used the term 'field' to refer to the Spirit of God.

The quantum realm resembles the spiritual domain, defined by its absence of shadows and its eternal nature. Consequently, if we are indeed spirit, as stated in the Bible, we exist within the timeless realm and manifest according to our thoughts. This suggests that we create matter from our mental images:

> *For as he thinks within himself, so he is.*
> Proverbs 23:7 NASB

Consequently, if our thoughts shape physical reality, as Einstein indicated, this also includes illness. It suggests that all material responds to an individual's beliefs, since, without time, all matter exists in the observer's mind. Jesus emphasizes this in the following verse:

> *Jesus said to him, "As far as possibilities go, everything is possible for the person who believes."*
> Mark 9:23 GWT

The spirit realm is an ocean of possibilities waiting on the combined energy of one's mind and heart in unison to change the unseen into the seen. If we really believe, then we already have what we believe even though we may not see it.

The quantum realm is analogous with the example of our noticing the number of cars like ours after we own it. In other words, they have always been there but gone unnoticed because our attention was elsewhere.

> *"That's why I tell you to have faith that you have already received whatever you pray for, and it will be yours."*
>
> Mark 11:24 GWT

This is the message of the kingdom that Jesus preached to His followers. There is nothing lacking for those who abide in His kingdom because matter follows the sole governing agent, which is you.

Simply put, all energy or spirit produces waves that create an invisible magnetic field. Think of a tornado as a representation of spirit, remaining unseen until surrounded by dust and debris. This illustrates how each human being appears, with their outer shape cloaked in the earthly matter pulled in by our thoughts and emotions.

Just as a tornado pulls in everything around it, our magnetic field attracts the things we focus on in this world. However, when we direct our attention to the unseen beauty of the present moment, we can enhance the attraction of what we truly need, often without even having to articulate it verbally.

This phenomenon arises from our focus on the fundamental essence of all things, rather than just the observable. It is indeed remarkable to recognize that God rewards those who consistently cultivate their faith by staying present.

> *Now without faith it is impossible to please Him, for the one who approaches God must believe that He exists and that He rewards those who seek Him.*
>
> Hebrews 11:6 NET

The true reward lies in remaining present, as Jesus noted in Matthew 6:33. When we redirect our attention from the visible to the invisible, prosperity flows seamlessly, like the act of breathing.

Our spirit truly understands the spiritual dimension and the truth it holds; yet, our conditioning often creates a sense of helplessness and need. In a similar way to a tornado gathering up nearby debris, our fears and doubts can pull in those thoughts, making them feel like a real part of our lives.

Begin your journey of being present today without getting caught up in doubts or unbelief, and you'll be amazed by the incredible power of the Holy Spirit as He draws everything you need to you.

DOCTRINES
BEWITCH

We recognize the significance of a proper foundation for discerning what to believe and why. Nothing is more vital for directing our actions than a firm grounding in the truth. Thus, when we are receptive to the Spirit of Truth, our senses will play a diminished role in decision making.

There is but one kingdom that rules both the invisible and visible realms: God's Kingdom. Although Adam's disobedience temporarily hindered its presence in this dimension until Christ's resurrection, it never forfeited its authority over the physical and spiritual realms.

There exist only two kingdoms, both of which are spiritual. The Kingdom of God, which is Christ, holds supreme authority over both kingdoms; however, the gift of free will permits individuals to choose between His Kingdom and the kingdom of this world. The foundation of this world's kingdom was established in Genesis 2:17 and Genesis 3:10.

> "except the tree that gives knowledge of what is good and what is bad. You must not eat the fruit of that tree; if you do, **you will die the same day**."
>
> Genesis 2:17 GNT

> He answered, "I heard You in the garden; **I was afraid** and hid from You, because I was naked."
>
> Genesis 3:17 GNT

The world is not just another term for Earth; God created all material things, including humans. He gave humans "free will" to shape their personal worlds. This is why today's physical dimension and its frequency result from Adam's choice.

The Earth was established as a habitat for a spiritual being to thrive and expand God's kingdom. Humanity was meant to live both *spiritually and physically*, reflecting Jesus as He walked the Earth. (Review the chapter on "Spiritually Physical")

Do you recall the scripture passages about Jesus walking through walls after His resurrection and the times His disciples failed to recognize Him? Many think this is due to Jesus' glorified body after resurrection and is also referred to in 1 Corinthians 15:44.

Humanity's misunderstanding of this has led many churches to misconstrue the concept of a "glorified body" as a future event. This highlights the confusion of people reading the Bible in its divided state today.

Not seeing people walk through walls or change appearances doesn't mean we can't. Jesus never shared the secrets of His kingdom with the masses. Our untransformed mind and dense bandwidth guarantees we will remain the same today as yesterday because we are too afraid to leave the known for the unknown.

Look inward for the validation of what Christ has purchased for us. If you believe something remains unfinished by His resurrection, you will follow the crowd and receive their reward. I have turned my gaze from the physical to focus on the invisible. The longer I maintain consciousness, the less time I spend searching for justifications to validate my current condition and beliefs. When I stopped perceiving what I had always considered to be true, the Holy Spirit revealed to me the truth. This is the only lens through which I observe this realm.

> *"You will know the truth, and the truth will set you free."*
>
> John 8:32 GWT

When we see ourselves solely as flesh rather than spirit, we set the stage for various inaccurate beliefs. This is why many messages become entangled in misunderstandings and misconceptions that foster doctrines founded on superstition and fear.

Our original dimension functions at a frequency that requires a higher bandwidth than what our mindset can perceive from birth in this realm. The sole obstacle to our daily awareness of that dimension is our belief, which is influenced by our current vibration and default beliefs.

To truly understand our freedom from this realm, both in mind and body, it's essential for us to be fully awake and aware. This awareness blossoms from our practice of non-judgmental mindfulness. By refraining from labeling our reactions to events and circumstances, we provide the spiritual energy that the Holy Spirit uses to assist in changing our mindset.

We often see ourselves as the sole judges of right and wrong. This mindset limits the Holy Spirit's ability to free us from our narrow views and assumptions accepted as truth due to our identity as "Christians." Such thinking drains our spiritual energy and confines our vibrational frequency to this limited dimension.

Jesus's single message was to seek the Kingdom of God. Yet today, churches around the world search for everything but His Kingdom. Why? Because humanity relies on the wisdom of this world to interpret the Bible.

> From that time Jesus began to preach and to say, **"Repent, for the kingdom of heaven is at hand."**
>
> Matthew 4:17 NKJ

Repentance involves more than simply experiencing guilt or regret for our errors; it represents a transformation in our mindset. However, this conversion occurs when we recognize our reactions to external influences that have been shaped by our conditioning.

Essentially, our automatic responses to the physical world tether us to the incorrect notion that we are solely physical beings, which further reinforces our reliance on our senses to affirm our material existence.

As we observe, we invite the Holy Spirit to transform our reactions, helping us awaken from the automatic patterns we've been conditioned to follow. This awareness becomes the light the Holy Spirit uses to deepen our understanding and awaken us from our conditioning.

It's important to remember that, initially, our primary role is simply to watch and be present.

A. DUALITY AND JUDGING ARE THE FRUIT OF FEAR

We understand that the foundation of this world system is built on the fear of death, and that eating from the wrong tree has fostered a mentality of duality throughout all creation. But have you considered that the fuel that keeps this way of thinking alive is really our tendency to judge?

The word judge is both a noun and a verb. God was and is the only Judge that operates in righteousness, which is the noun. The use of the word as a verb is illustrated by Jesus in the following verse:

> *"Stop judging so that you will not be judged.*
>
> *Otherwise, you will be judged by the same standard you use to judge others. The standards you use for others will be applied to you."*
>
> Matthew 7:1-2 GWT

Jesus explains that this realm responds to God's creation as if He were speaking. All creation comes from Him and behaves according to His thoughts and words because it is part of Him.

In essence, He is not detached from His thoughts, words, or feelings. Nothing He creates exists separately unless it voluntarily separates from the

Oneness of God. Free will is a fundamental aspect of God's righteousness. Faith is the fruit of love because without faith, nothing would come into existence.

Viewing creation as separate from the Creator leads to internal separation, causing us to judge ourselves. This prompts Jesus' warning against self-condemnation and highlights God as the Righteous Judge.

Essentially, judgment and various forms of separation deplete our spiritual energy, much like they did for Adam when he chose to disobey. This depletion occurs whenever we sever our connection to our oneness in Him. Jesus cautioned against judgment because He desires our unity with Him.

B. THE REAL PURPOSE OF THE LAW

The divine laws from God protected Israel in the wilderness and established Jesus' lineage. Most religions share roots in the Old Testament, even if their sacred texts are the Quran, Vedas, Bhagavad Gita, or The Rig Veda. The "duality mindset" is universal, forming the basis of the Law, leading God to establish His law in this world.

The duality mindset anchored in the tree of knowledge has persisted across generations. While the Mosaic law portrays God as the Supreme Judge, contemporary views assign this role to humanity, leading to a recurrence of corruption and injustice.

The Old Testament laws illustrate the dynamics between Roman Emperors and the Jewish Priesthood, highlighting the influence of religion on the world system. These principles have now been adapted to explain why the contemporary world mirrors Jerusalem prior to the Temple's destruction in 70 AD.

Many new believers in contemporary churches are unaware that in 70 AD, Jerusalem faced "the" tribulation as Jesus foretold. The valley was filled with blood up to the horses' necks. For a detailed account, I recommend my wife's book, *The End of An Era*.

The Rabbis, Pharisees, and Sadducees viewed Jesus as a danger and disregarded His teachings, becoming the loudest advocates for His crucifixion. Additionally, their true motivation for wanting Jesus dead stemmed from their preference for mammon as their god. The following verse backs up this assertion and was used as the primary charge against Him during the trial before Pilate.

> *This fellow said,* **"I am able to destroy the temple of God and to build it in three days."**
>
> Matthew 26:61 NKJ

The law was God's strategy to dismantle satan's dominion and restore His kingdom on Earth. While satan tried to misrepresent righteousness through God's Law, he overlooked its directive for capital punishment for unjust killings. Thus,

Jesus, the Innocent One, was wrongfully executed by satan, resulting in his eternal condemnation in the lake of fire.

The sin consciousness from Adam is the cornerstone of this world; however, the following verse shows God always knew the end from the beginning.

> *"Father, they are Your gift to Me; and My desire is that they may be with Me where I am, so that they may look upon My glory, which You have given Me because You loved Me before the world began."*
>
> John 17:24 GWT

This love embodies God's faith present in all who are in Him since the world's foundation. To free yourself from the anxieties Jesus warned about in John 16:33, remember His faith created everything you seek and resides within us. It's easy to forget our identity by seeking what we believe we lack. Reflect on this.

The Holy Spirit revealed that the Bible's division was not God's intention but the result of willful ignorance or lack of understanding of the power from Christ's resurrection. This power restores us to wholeness in Him, yet your free will either draws you closer or pushes you farther from that reality.

The Bible illustrates humanity's and satan's destiny in Revelation, marking a pivotal time that fulfills God's prophecy in Genesis. This highlights the need to view the Bible as a unified work instead of separating it into the Old and New Testaments. It's a pity that the spiritual and physical impacts of that often go unnoticed by those who depend on others to explain the scriptures and create doctrines, which can unintentionally nurture an anti-Christ spirit among their followers.

For example, consider the foundation of the United States, which is proudly proclaimed to be Judeo-Christian. Examine what that declaration means; despite its seemingly holy sound, it is, in fact, anti-Christ.

The Judeo-Christians believe in the God of Abraham, Isaac, and Jacob. They also believe in Yeshua (Jesus), who is the Messiah of Israel. They also **believe Yeshua is the Messiah of Israel, and He will fulfill all the Scriptures that have been prophesied about Him concerning Israel**.

The issue with this declaration is clear. They doubt Jesus fulfilled His divine mission, including the Temple's destruction. This heretical assertion underpins many beliefs in the United States and reflects views held by most Christians and churches.

The repercussions of this situation are more insidious than you might think. The continuing strife in the Middle East is the destiny of any nation that associates with an anti-Christ spirit. Achieving peace on earth is impossible if humanity continues to deny the truth of Christ.

CHAPTER 9 ▎DOCTRINES BEWITCH

The most notable example of heresy, from my perspective, pertains to the doctrine concerning His death and resurrection. Jesus stated the following to those who questioned His legitimacy as the Son of God.

> *Then He was accosted by some of the Scribes and of the Pharisees who said, "Teacher, we wish to see a sign given by you."*
>
> *"Wicked and faithless generation!" He replied, "they clamor for a sign, but none shall be given to them except the sign of the Prophet Jonah."*
>
> *"For just as JONAH WAS THREE DAYS IN THE SEA-MONSTER'S BELLY, so will the Son of Man be three days in the heart of the earth."*
>
> Matthew 12:38-40 WEY

Jesus faced ongoing challenges from the Jewish authorities, who demanded that He provide signs and wonders to prove His claim of being the Messiah. He clearly stated that His death and resurrection would serve as the only sign validating His identity as the Son of God, likening it to Jonah's experience of three days and nights in the depths of the earth.

My religious upbringing emphasized the observance of "Good Friday" as the day commemorating the crucifixion of Jesus, followed by His resurrection on

Sunday morning. However, this perspective does not align with the full duration of three days and three nights. What explains this discrepancy? In my view, it stems from the influence of an anti-Christ spirit that shaped religion and the design of the Bible.

It's astonishing that a significant number of Christians, despite having access to printed or digital Bibles, continue to hold the belief that Jesus was crucified and laid to rest on Good Friday, only to rise again on Sunday morning.

This lie began around 300 A.D. by the Roman emperor Constantine to force followers of Jesus Christ to adopt paganism and idolatry as Christianity. Thus, Constantine and the Council of Nicaea stated that Jesus was crucified and buried on Good Friday and resurrected on Easter Sunday.

Millions of Christians adopted this doctrine without searching the Bible. Today we have access to the original facts and the original instructions and are capable of basic calculations. Sadly, if one believes this lie what is to prevent them from believing others?

If you want a deeper dive into this and other truths, read my book, *Who Has Bewitched You*?

Unless we alter our conscious awareness and challenge our beliefs and their reasons, our foundation will mirror this worldly system, and the outcome will reflect what we read in the Old Testament.

Challenging and reexamining our understanding of Christ is crucial to revealing His kingdom. If our reality fails to mirror His resurrection in our lives, the fear of death will influence our perceptions and decisions.

The energy we utilize to remain present allows the Holy Spirit to reveal our condition. Following His involvement, your perception and response to physical stimuli will undergo a significant transformation.

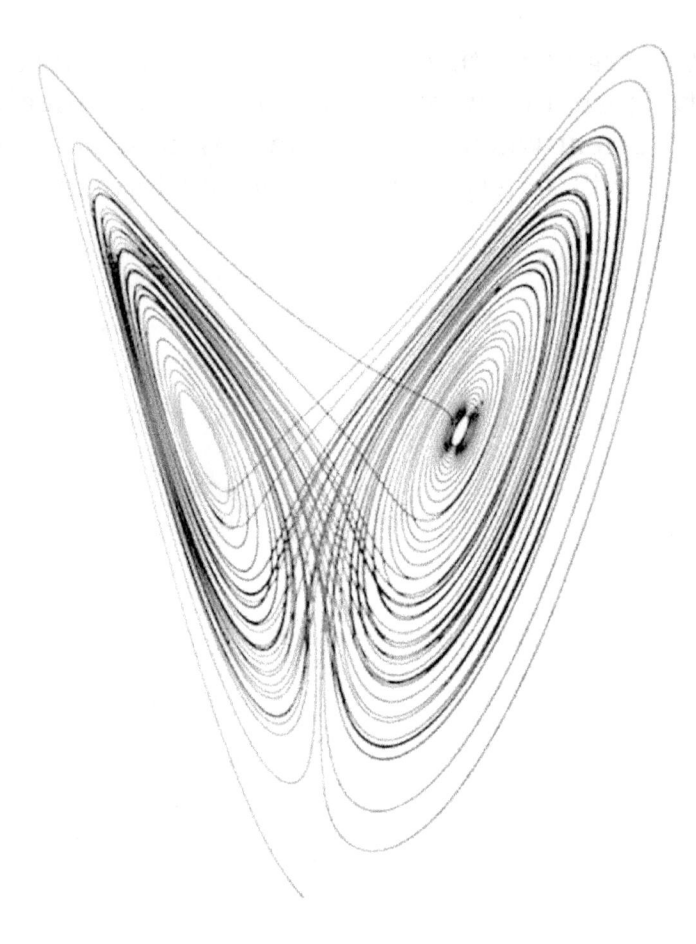

THE ANTI-CHRIST SPIRIT

The anti-Christ spirit originated in the Garden when Adam refused to believe God, which allowed satan rulership over the second heaven. The power of the anti-Christ spirit was eliminated through the resurrection of Christ, but the source of that power is the fear of death, which constitutes the foundation of this world. Consequently, individuals who decline to enter God's kingdom will encounter the doctrines and theologies of that spirit within this world's system, despite the fact that the origin of that spirit resides in hell.

This is why it is vital to comprehend that a covenant with Jesus does not exempt us from the subliminal messages present within the world's system governed by the beliefs of the anti-Christ spirit. However, it is essential to understand that doctrines are powerless unless they are believed in.

The United States proudly identifies as a Judeo-Christian nation. This claim resonates with those whose religious leaders interpret the Gospels as part of the New Testament, even though Jesus clearly defines one of His key purposes for coming to Earth:

> *"Do not for a moment suppose that I have come to abolish the Law or the Prophets: I have not come to abolish them but to give them their completion."*
>
> Matthew 5:17 WEY

Consequently, as mentioned in a previous chapter, Judeo-Christians believe that Jesus is the Messiah; however, they argue that His mission is not fulfilled until, as per their doctrine, "all" of Israel recognizes Him as the Messiah.

This ignorance fuels the bewitching of religious doctrines and mainstream views. The scriptures below confirm that Jesus fulfilled His assignment:

> *After this Jesus, knowing that all things are now finished, that the scripture might be accomplished, saith, "I thirst."*

> *There was set there a vessel full of vinegar: so they put a sponge full of the vinegar upon hyssop, and brought it to His mouth.*
>
> *When Jesus therefore had received the vinegar, He said, "It is finished:" and He bowed His head, and gave up His spirit.*
>
> John 19:28-30 ERV

In verse 28, Jesus references the prophecy found in Psalm 69:21, which states, *"They also gave me gall for my food, and for my thirst they gave me vinegar to drink."* Jesus has fulfilled all prophecies concerning Himself.

This indicates that there is nothing further to be accomplished. Therefore, the division of the Bible is a "human-constructed deception" intended to mislead and manipulate individuals.

The reality of the book we call the Bible is that it is one book inspired by the Holy Spirit to provoke those in Him before the foundation of the world to remember their origin.

The scriptures are designed to reveal God's love and the fulfillment of His prophecy in the Garden, where He declared that He would crush the serpent and, in doing so, reunite humanity with Himself in Oneness.

When reflecting on the crucifixion and resurrection of Jesus, it is crucial to recognize that neither the

Bible nor social media was available to convey this profound shift in consciousness, both in the heavens and on Earth.

Viewing Jesus' return as essential due to the suffering inflicted on His followers by the devil places us alongside those who awaited their Messiah under the law. If we believe that the devil, as an uncontrollable force, impacts our lives, we remain in the Babylon from which Jesus urged us to escape.

The truth is that we are truly liberated! However, as long as our lives remain connected to the material world, they will naturally reflect the worldly system and its resonant frequency, much like the times when Jesus walked the earth.

■ TWO ASSIGNMENTS ONE GOAL: WHOLENESS

Prior to His crucifixion and resurrection, Jesus received two key assignments. First, He was to complete the Law that predicted His divine birth.

Second, His mission was to reinstate God's invisible kingdom among all believers, thus overcoming satan's dominion over the thoughts and hearts of humanity.

Essentially, those in Him before the foundation of the world became God's Ark of the Covenant, which, similar to its role in the desert, dispelled evil simply by existing.

I became convinced and shifted my focus inward rather than looking for physical proof of God's rule in the world. Right away, the Holy Spirit led me to the verse in John 3:3 and instructed me not to stop searching until I witness His Kingdom.

> *Jesus answered, "I am telling you the truth: no one can see the Kingdom of God without being born again."*
>
> John 3:3

This search produced the book, "*Immersed In Him.*" If you haven't studied it, you may find my language and communication difficult to comprehend at first.

I've encountered many individuals who have gone through profoundly difficult experiences marked by trauma, leading them to feel imprisoned. It's clear that no mere words can change their perceptions or beliefs about their situations.

This occurs because they see themselves as victims of circumstances beyond their control. In reality, change becomes attainable when a person starts to recognize their role in their circumstances.

Our ability as creators to influence circumstances should be a key takeaway from this book.

You are embarking on a transformative journey that will fundamentally alter your beliefs. However, if we persist in the notion that trauma obstructs our progress, we will inevitably carry that belief along with its accompanying emotions and pain. Moreover, the longer we identify with that experience, the more challenging it becomes to acknowledge the truth of what Christ redeemed during the resurrection.

A large segment of the global population suffers from physical or mental distress as a consequence of their decision to follow the wisdom of the worldly system instead of being led by The Spirit.

Old Testament teachings frequently influence individuals who deny that Jesus accomplished His divine missions. This can unintentionally promote a link with the antichrist spirit, which perpetuates a victim mentality.

Many churches highlight scripture where Jesus warns of tribulation. Congregations view this as a future event, particularly due to the Bible's division into Old and New Testaments.

The Gospels fulfill God's covenant with Israel and the Law of Moses. Teaching differently promotes an antichrist spirit, which weakens Christ's power and authority today. This heresy arose during Jesus' time, leading the apostles to warn against the antichrist spirit.

> *Who is a liar? Who else but the person who rejects Jesus as the Messiah? The person who rejects the Father and the Son is an antichrist.*
>
> 1 John 2:22 GWT

Humans rely on their senses to affirm their beliefs, which is why the phrase "seeing is believing" exists. Paul noted that the Jews sought miraculous signs, while the Greeks pursued wisdom.

Miraculous events exceed scientific understanding, captivating us and drawing many to congregations that claim to provide evidence. Modern churches, similar to the synagogues of Jesus' time, attract those seeking His miraculous signs. Generally, people search for supernatural solutions only after they have exhausted all physical remedies for their problems.

Depending on tangible evidence to affirm intangible experiences blurs the line between the Israelites in the desert and the modern church. This tendency shifts people's attention towards material elements for sensory validation, intensifying the fear of death that worsens their situation.

This presents a challenge we must face, especially if we aim to nurture a significant relationship with the risen Christ and deeply engage with the miraculous kingdom of God in our everyday lives.

The law illustrated God's covenant, showcasing His power and salvation; however, it was not the ultimate covenant. Consequently, what was intended to foster a personal covenant with the resurrected Christ transformed into a religious basis for the antichrist spirit, as mentioned in 1 John 2:22.

God's law operates on multiple levels; it defeated satan and paved the way for Christ to restore His kingdom. Jesus fulfilled God's law to establish a personal covenant with us.

■ IN MY OPINION

This section reflects my viewpoint and is not intended to criticize or judge differing beliefs. It's important to recognize that my goal in sharing this perspective is to provide personal insights for those who genuinely love the Lord but find it challenging to fully accept the freedom given by Christ. I base the following on my own experiences.

First, let me clarify the reference to a second heaven. I use this term to describe the dimension satan controlled before Jesus's crucifixion and resurrection. I believe this is the realm mentioned by Paul in his letter to the Ephesians.

> *that there might be made known now to the principalities and the authorities in the heavenly [places], through the assembly, the manifold wisdom of God,*
>
> Ephesians 3:10 YLT

> *because we have not the wrestling with blood and flesh, but with the principalities, with the authorities, with the world-rulers* **of the darkness of this age***, with the spiritual things of the evil in the heavenly places;*
>
> Ephesians 6:12 YLT

Paul is sharing with his followers that his mission during that time was to bring light to the Gentiles through the message of the resurrection. They were a people and nation shaped by their imaginations and thoughts, which I believe resembled those who were killed in the flood.

When Adam gave up authority, God lost His mental link to influence the physical world. As God's Son on Earth, Adam reflected His thoughts of love and unity, connecting heaven and earth. This responsibility now lies with His living New Testament, encompassing everyone in covenant with the risen Christ.

The loss of that position allowed the deceiver to instill doubt, unbelief, and death, leading to a mental and physical virus called sin. If unchecked, sin could destroy God's creation. Consequently, all flesh was wiped out by a flood, solving the physical problem but not the mental condition.

This mentality is the default condition at birth, but thanks to Jesus, it doesn't have to be permanent! Understanding this is crucial, which is precisely why I'm writing this book.

As previously mentioned, the second heaven represents the dimension where our imagination shapes our thoughts and beliefs. Consequently, as a result of the influence of the "liar," fear, doubt, and unbelief have been mentally instilled in every generation.

Therefore, it's no surprise that humanity has persistently pursued wars and conflicts, a fact echoed in the scriptures of Ecclesiastes.

> *Whatever has happened before will happen "again". Whatever has been done before will be done "again". There is nothing new under the sun.*
>
> Ecclesiastes 1:9 GWT

Additionally, this is the reason why the inhabitants are conditioned to fear death. The prevalence of death and lack of belief deteriorate human beings, as this vibration emits a virus that resonates with the spirit of the anti-Christ, which ultimately destroys the soul and distorts beliefs and perceptions. Jesus was sent to save the souls of humanity through His Father's sacrifice.

> **"The time of judgment for the world has come—and the time when satan,* the prince of this world, shall be cast out."**
>
> John 12:31 LB

That era ended with Christ's resurrection, concluding satan's dominion in that dimension. The term "the second heaven" refers to our minds, the seat of free will. Our authority as creators allows us to manifest our beliefs, imaginations, and fears from that realm.

Remaining at the foot of the cross and worshiping God for Jesus reflects the early believers' viewpoint, who were unaware that Christ's resurrection raised us to heavenly realms, far beyond the mental frequencies considered normal in this dimension.

Please don't think for a second that I am undermining the importance of the cross. It played a crucial role in God's plan to eliminate satan from both heaven and earth. **Presently, he exists with Lucifer in the lake of fire.**

> *Whoever continues to sin belongs to the Devil, because the Devil has sinned from the very beginning.* **The Son of God appeared for this very reason, to destroy what the Devil had done.**
>
> 1 John 3:8 TEV

If Christ completed His work, which I firmly believe He did, that implies He obliterated the works of the devil, which originated in the Garden with unbelief. **The power to change your condition is your free will to do without any interference from the devil or demons.**

I understand the early church's focus on expelling demons and freeing people from satan. At that time, demons worked through those Paul and the disciples encountered because the world was in darkness for thousands of years and had not yet realized that "the light" had arrived to defeat the works of the devil through the resurrection. Evidence indicates that even the disciples struggled to fully grasp the authority given to them through His resurrection.

After I consciously entered a covenant with Christ, my perspective shifted, and I realized I am indeed the New Testament. This realization revealed that death has been conquered, freeing me from the worldly system governed by the fear of death, which the devil propagated before Christ. Additionally, I am in control of my will; otherwise, God would have destroyed satan in the Garden and forced us to believe Him.

I am merely sharing my personal experience. My conviction that I am the New Testament provides me with the most liberating feeling on earth and grants me access to His dimensions as never before. Furthermore, for me, the devil holds no authority over my free will because I believe Jesus defeated him, as clearly stated in the verse in Hebrews:

> *Since all of these sons and daughters have flesh and blood, Jesus took on flesh and blood to be like them.* **He did this so that by dying he would destroy the one who had power over death (that is, the devil).**
>
> ***In this way he would free those who were slaves all their lives because they were afraid of dying.***
>
> Hebrews 2:14-15 GWT

Throughout history, individuals have held the view that they are not responsible for their physical well-being due to the influence of supernatural forces that dominate them. This belief forms the foundation of most religious establishments, which, in my opinion, are in covenant with Jesus of Nazareth.

Individuals who persist in that state will encounter the same confrontational mentality that the disciples experienced during the earthly ministry of Jesus. Why is this the case? Because Jesus had not yet been crucified or resurrected. Jesus stated, *"I finished the works,"* which included the destruction of the works of the devil. However, each person must determine their own beliefs and the reasons behind them.

The power of resurrection reveals our origin beyond this dimension, where faith endures and angels submit to our authority because we are in Him. Our life begins when we lose our identity and enter into a covenant with the risen Christ.

A significant turning point for me was understanding my covenant with Jesus of Nazareth did not change the way I thought. It was not until I entered the resurrected Christ that I remembered my origin in Him. This realization opened my spiritual eyes to a dimension I experience daily.

If I can do it, so can you, starting when you decide you are the master of your free will and destiny.

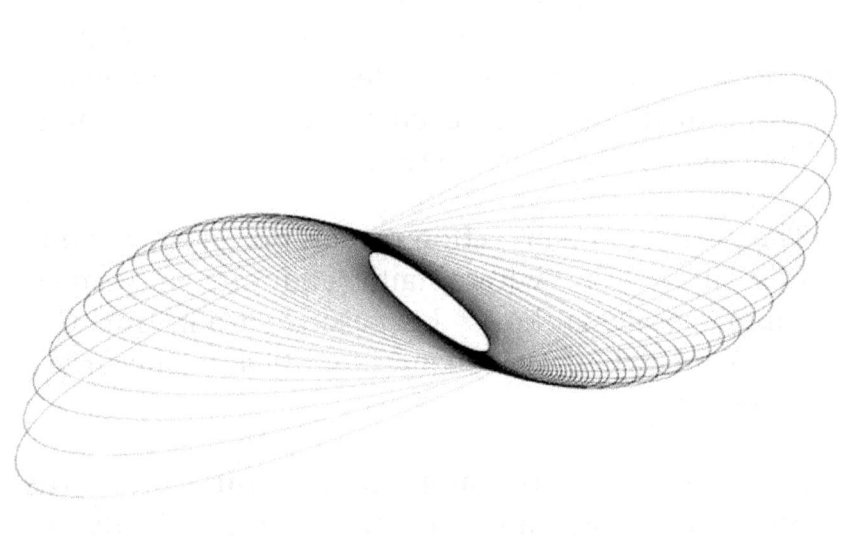

CHAPTER 11

RESONANCE OF BABYLON

Babylon is the Greek form of BABEL; Semitic form Babilu, meaning "The Gate of God." In the Assyrian tablets it means "The city of the dispersion of the tribes." The list of its kings goes as far back as B.C. 2300, and includes Khammurabi, or Amraphel is the contemporary of Abraham.

There's so much to explore about the significance of that country and its remarkable king, Nebuchadnezzar. To put it simply, God selected Nebuchadnezzar as a unique instrument to set the default frequency for our world system.

Babylon is known as the first kingdom to destroy Jerusalem and is represented as the golden head of the statue in Nebuchadnezzar's dream with Daniel. This statue symbolizes all earthly kingdoms, with the head symbolizing an anti-Christ figure.

In other words, the mentality of Babylon fostered behaviors such as pride, arrogance, self-reliance, greed, godlessness, materialism, idolatry, social injustice, and judgment. The depiction of gold as the head symbolizes the profound significance of the mind as humanity's most treasured asset.

Consequently, portraying this mentality as the resonant vibration underpinning the foundation of this world system should raise significant concerns for those seeking human wisdom over the mind of Christ.

God used Babylon as a tool to both destroy and judge Israel by capturing its people and destroying Jerusalem, including its temple. This captivity caused much more devastation than just imprisonment. The mentality of Babylon became so entrenched in the Israelites that, after their release, they exhibited a similar antichrist attitude within the context of the Mosaic laws.

This mindset gave rise to the Pharisees and Sadducees, paving the way for Christ's crucifixion. Readers of Revelation who approach the text with spiritual insight quickly realize that Jerusalem is depicted as Babylon. The scriptures below refer to this "great city," which we identify as Jerusalem.

CHAPTER 11 | RESONANCE OF BABYLON

*And another angel followed, saying, "Babylon is fallen, is fallen, **that great city**, because she has made all nations drink of the wine of the wrath of her fornication."*

Revelation 14:8 NKJV

*And their dead bodies will lie in the street of **the great city which spiritually is called Sodom and Egypt, where also our Lord was crucified.***

Revelation 11:8 NKJV

John demonstrates the link between Rome, the global system, and the religious framework of Judaism as depicted in the following verses.

The verses below exemplifies the model embraced by all world systems. It portrays the Harlot, symbolizing Jerusalem, riding atop the governance of Rome to fulfill God's mission to destroy all who think like Babylon:

Then he carried me away in spirit to a deserted place where I saw a woman seated on a scarlet beast that was covered with blasphemous names, with seven heads and ten horns.

The woman was wearing purple and scarlet and adorned with gold, precious stones, and pearls. She held

> *in her hand a gold cup that was filled with the abominable and sordid deeds of her harlotry.*
>
> *On her forehead was written a name, which is a mystery, "Babylon the great, the mother of harlots and of the abominations of the earth."*
>
> *I saw that the woman was drunk on the blood of the holy ones and on the blood of the witnesses to Jesus.*
>
> Revelation 17:3-6 NAB

This accurately reflects the current global system. Political systems and religion manifest the mentality or frequency transmitted to God's chosen people by Babylon, proliferating like a virus worldwide. Naturally, it has had to evolve into thousands, if not millions, of variations and cultures to sustain itself within civilizations.

Religion plays a crucial role in society by maintaining control; however, for it to be effective, the populace must live in fear. This is why most church systems emphasize the physical realm as reality, with all its chaos and impending disasters.

This model reinforces the use of the Old Testament, guiding its followers to evaluate all physical material through the lens of the law. Nothing divides more swiftly than judging right and wrong as the law does.

The world system's core essence is the fear of death, driving all atoms to express themselves through this mindset, manifesting chaos that this belief attracts, creating a never-ending cycle resonating within the frequency of death.

Jesus fulfilled the Law by embodying God's presence on Earth, reestablishing humanity's connection to the Creator. However, each generation seeks signs and wonders as evidence of God's existence.

This reflects the same anti-Christ spirit that was present during His time, which has generated a distinct frequency in today's world system. We will discuss that subject in detail soon.

Frequency acts as the nonverbal language of creation, with resonance occurring between objects whose atoms vibrate at the same frequencies. For example, striking a tuning fork tuned to C makes all objects in that key vibrate similarly.

Every thought generates energy that affects atoms, producing vibrations. Thus, when many individuals express similar thoughts, they create a vibration that reflects the resonant frequency or collective consciousness of their community. A notable example of this phenomenon is observed in the recorded frequencies of Earth and human beings.

The Earth resonates at 7.83 Hz, while resting humans measure about 7.5 Hz, underscoring the deep connection between people and the planet. Humanity is called to care for this Earth, which demands a harmonious alignment with all life.

Jesus linked repentance to the approaching kingdom, requiring a specific mindset. This understanding underpinned His call for people to flee Babylon, as noted in Revelation 18:4.

> *I heard another voice from heaven saying, **"Come out of Babylon**, my people, so that you do not participate in her sins and suffer from any of her plagues.*
>
> Revelation 18:4

Furthermore, in the subsequent verse, God brought about the destruction of Jerusalem due to its spiritual resonance with the frequency of the Antichrist. This holds considerable significance for those who are convinced that they can alter this system. This system will perpetually embody the Antichrist system as a consequence of Adam's choice.

> *Their dead bodies will lie on the street of the great city that is spiritually called Sodom and Egypt, where also their Lord was crucified.*
>
> Revelation 11:8 CEB

Change in this system starts from within, beginning with our attention. Shifting our focus to the present prevents our minds from lingering on the past or future. This small adjustment influences the energy we emit and absorb.

The frequency of humanity on this planet mirrors that of a person in a state of sleepwalking. Nevertheless, the Holy Spirit is constantly presenting opportunities to experience higher frequencies to replace the default vibrations we unconsciously obtained in childhood.

Individuals often choose paths to predict their futures, stemming from a global system rooted in the fear of death. By forecasting outcomes, people think they can shield themselves from this fear, but this illusion of security restricts our ability to embrace the unknown.

Creation unfolds and transforms, revealing secrets often unnoticed in our unconscious. Observing eternity in the present helps us understand that His love surpasses our fears. Relaxing in this knowledge allows our needs to be met in extraordinary ways, as provision exists now, not in the future.

The Bible serves as the primary guide to illustrate the outcomes of pursuing any doctrine or mindset that reflects an anti-Christ spirit. Understanding the Bible as a cohesive text will enable the Holy Spirit to radically transform your ability to live as sons of God.

> *And Jesus, full of the Holy Spirit, returned from the Jordan, and was led by the Spirit in the wilderness.*
>
> Luke 4:1 ERV

For as many as are led by the Spirit of God, these are sons of God.

Romans 8:14 ERV

But if ye are led by the Spirit, ye are not under the law.

Galatians 5:18 ERV

CHAPTER 11 RESONANCE OF BABYLON

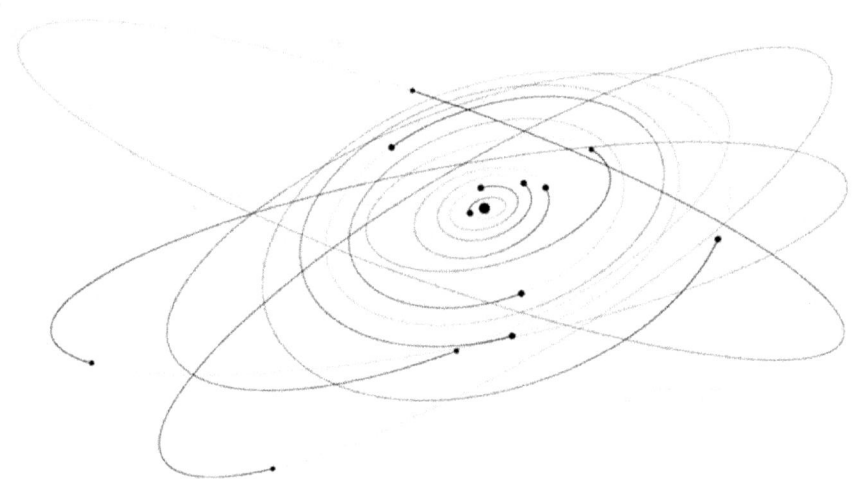

THE BIBLE
WITHOUT DIVISION

Separation and division significantly distract us from connecting with God's Spirit. One main reason we may experience this disconnection is our quest for something we perceive as lacking.

For instance, when we desire something like a car, job, house, or fame, it's easy to justify that feeling of lack based on a superficial assessment of our situation. Our senses and emotions serve as tools to evaluate our physical condition and affirm our motivations.

Every pursuit in this dimension has value when we are aware of our actions and intentions. It's important to listen, as this is significant! Our physical state reflects our desire to embrace this realm as His beautiful creation filled with love. Jesus died and was resurrected due to God's immense love for us. Love is the fruit of faith; God believes in and loves you—His creation—without judgment or punishment.

All parents want the best for their children because of their love and faith in them. We also want to protect them without controlling them, even though we know their choices may lead to heartache and misery.

Our Father in heaven operates in the same way, but His perspective is multi-generational. This means we have no end in Him because we are spiritual, while this material dimension is entirely linear.

Therefore, if we are taught this from an early age, our desire to achieve the perspective of our heavenly Father will outweigh our craving to experience linear material devoid of substance.

This tendency is most evident among those who recognize the power of unity in thought and feeling. The ability to remain focused on the present moment diminishes the desire to detach from the whole and resist the illusion of substance as reality.

This chapter reveals the power of oneness that describes God. Man was created as both male and female, illustrating God's order and purpose for living in Him, as Paul describes in Ephesians 1:4.

> *just as He chose us in Him before the foundation of the world, that we should be holy and without blame before Him in love,*
>
> Ephesians 1:4

The challenge in understanding this truth stems from our conditioning and tendency to fear what we cannot predict or control, particularly the present moment.

The enduring power of the Bible's written word comes from its spiritual origin, which unites us. Additionally, the supernatural captivates us because of our belief in its authenticity.

Furthermore, the truth in the scriptures is a divine force that reminds us that our source is God, who is love. The Bible serves as the testament that God chose to document the most incredible love story ever told.

> *God so loved the world that He gave His only Son, so everyone who believes in Him won't perish but will have eternal life.*
>
> John 3:16 KJV

The Bible recounts God's remarkable birth, life, death, and resurrection through Jesus. This is the manifestation of God's prophecy found in Genesis 3.

> *And I will put enmity between you and the woman, and between your offspring and her Offspring;* **He will bruise and tread your head underfoot, and you will lie in wait and bruise His heel.**
>
> Genesis. 3:15 AMP

God's prophecy is fulfilled through covenants and miracles over millennia, preserving the stories until documented in the Bible. Many things were concealed from angels, and as John 21:25 states, the world cannot contain all that Jesus accomplished.

> *God revealed to the prophets that the things they had spoken were not for their own benefit but for yours. What the prophets had spoken, the Holy Spirit, who was sent from heaven, has now made known to you by those who spread the Good News among you.* **These are things that even the angels want to look into.**
>
> 1 Peter 1:12 GWT

> *But there are also many other things which Jesus did—so vast a number indeed that if they were all described in detail,* **I suppose that the world itself could not contain the books** *that would have to be written.*
>
> John 21:25 WEY

■ FREQUENCY OF TRUTH

The power of prophecy lies not in the physical words but in the spiritual atmosphere their vibrations create. The frequency of eternity that resides in Christ's word compels matter to transform and manifest what is spoken.

Here is something you must understand. Reading written words is not the same as hearing the person being quoted. Why? Sound is multidimensional, whereas written words are two-dimensional.

To truly grasp the essence of God's written word, our eyes and ears must resonate with the frequency of love. Love and faith exist within the timeless bandwidth of eternity, which is why scripture should not be viewed through a linear lens.

Fear and duality resonate within this world system, which compels one to discern right from wrong. Truth is a frequency that establishes itself through love, which is God, the only Righteous Judge. Truth is what draws us back to our origin.

The Bible unfolds dynamically after the Word God speaks in Genesis 1:3, empowering the void to become the finished work before time. The eternal realm is endless; thus, God's Word is, was, and will always be the beginning and end of all things visible and invisible.

The Bible we read today uses words within this dimension to translate and interpret spiritual concepts aimed at describing the creation of all material things, which requires their separation.

God separated the woman from man, and the waters from the waters. This separation was meant to be temporary until evil could be judged. Our revelation of Christ must ultimately lead us back to oneness in Him.

The greater this revelation grows inside our spirit, the more powerful our attention to the eternal present moment becomes because that is the place of both wholeness and rest in God.

The scriptures have profoundly shaped my journey with Christ. Approaching the Bible as a unified text, without separating the Old and New Covenants, offers a rich, multidimensional experience.

This implies that genuine spiritual transformation necessitates unity, achieved only when we avoid dividing it into the Old and New Testaments. Viewing it as a whole invokes a transformative mental shift. For instance, most works classified as the "New Testament" are authored by Paul.

Paul had access only to the Tenakh, which consisted of 24 books from the Old Testament.

This highlights that every letter written by Paul references Old Covenant scriptures that are fulfilled by Jesus. The New Testament introduces nothing new.

The division of the Bible was intended to keep people separated and dependent on religion rather than on the Holy Spirit.

I believe the Bible is a unified text inspired by the Holy Spirit to awaken those in Him before the world was formed by the sin consciousness of Adam.

Paul discovered Jesus in the Spirit through those sacred texts, which fulfill the purpose of the Bible. His letter to Timothy demonstrates that all scriptures are spiritually inspired and intended to transform the destiny of anyone seeking the truth.

> *and that from infancy, you have known the sacred writings that can **make you wise and help you obtain salvation through faith in Christ Jesus.***
>
> ***Every Scripture is inspired by God** and is useful for teaching, for convincing, for correction of error, and for instruction in right doing.*
>
> 2 Timothy 3:15-16 WEY

Therefore, the Bible is, in fact, man's attempt at reproducing God's words spoken into this dimension. Unfortunately, because the human race is born into Adam's sin consciousness, the interpretations are divided into books, chapters, verses, and the Old and New Testaments.

This does not make the Bible irrelevant or unimportant; rather, it demonstrates the power of the spiritual realm over this dimension, despite the misinterpretations and divisions reflected by the multitude of denominations.

Religion has always been a man-made phenomenon stemming from our limited knowledge of our spiritual origins. Consequently, there have been countless wars and bloodshed, all in the name of religion.

Nevertheless, even with its current configurations and interpretations, the power of the divine resonates to draw those who are "IN HIM" before the foundation of the world.

The Old Testament contains the highest number of books in the Bible. Although there are various reasons for this, many agree that its primary purpose is to provide genealogical proof of the Messiah's lineage and to prophetically map out the historical events leading to the birth of Jesus Christ.

Each book serves as a prophetic journal meant to illustrate what I believe is the only physical event on Earth that acts as a gateway to God's invisible kingdom.

Christ's birth, death, and resurrection are undeniably the most significant moments in history, fundamentally altering humanity's trajectory. While discussions about the specifics of these events may

CHAPTER 12 | THE BIBLE WITHOUT DIVISION

arise, nothing in the physical realm will ever compare to Christ's reestablishment of His kingdom here.

In truth, the Old Covenant was not just fulfilled; Christ's resurrection transformed this material world permanently. This idea is hard to accept if we continue to be bound by the religious laws of Moses.

The Spirit wrote the Bible for spiritual beings, making it unpopular with intellectuals and difficult for those reliant on their senses. However, our origin as spirits is vital, granting us the unique opportunity to be guided by a willing Holy Spirit.

The conflict between trusting the visible and the invisible has existed since creation, culminating in a flood that preserved Noah's lineage. Even though Noah's family survived, sin remained inherent in all born on Earth due to God's commitment to free will.

Sin is the force that brings about physical death in this dimension. It's not your actions that constitute sin, but rather your beliefs, and we quickly discovered that God's first creation did not believe in Him.

The core message of the Bible emanates from a divine love and majesty that transcends human concepts of salvation through grace, culminating in the resurrected Christ.

This is the secret of spiritually walking in the flesh while perceiving and hearing our Heavenly Father. Those who recognize this are the true Sons of God and have embraced the wholeness in God.

While many acknowledge that Jesus conquered death, others find it hard to accept that their true essence—the spirit—also shared in this victory with Christ. Death instills fear in many; yet, if you have already died with Jesus, there is no reason to fear.

For your faith to prevail over fear, this awareness must transition from a mere concept to a solid foundation that starts with our thinking. Unbelief creates our fear, which stems from the sin consciousness we inherit at birth.

Our mindset shifts once we understand our spiritual essence, which is realized at the cross. This process requires the death of our own image, just as Jesus did. Nevertheless, our image stems from our belief that we are not one with God.

Jesus became the Christ by fulfilling God's mandate as the sinless man. On the cross, He made a covenant with His Father to uphold the law and restore God's Kingdom on earth through His presence as The Christ.

> *God made a promise to Abraham. Since He had no one greater on whom to base His oath, He based it on Himself.*
>
> Hebrews 6:13 GWT

Do you recall that when God established a covenant with Abraham, He made that covenant with Himself to guarantee its permanence? This is precisely what Christ achieved at the resurrection.

It is crucial to highlight that we witnessed that moment before taking on human form. Paul expresses this in Ephesians 1:4, asserting that we existed in Him before the world's foundation.

Abraham, known as the "father of faith," exemplified God's kingdom on earth by aligning his heart and mind with God. He embodied the covenant that God established with humanity through Himself.

Nevertheless, it foreshadowed the covenant He would establish with each of us who enters into a relationship with the resurrected Christ. This is significant because today's religions encourage their followers to form a covenant with Jesus of Nazereth. That covenant is essential for salvation, but places us firmly inside the Babylonian system of this world's system.

God's remarkable aim in concluding His temporary covenants was to establish a perpetual covenant within every individual. This invites us to embrace a truly new perspective that transcends our earthly existence.

Jesus urged His followers to seek and enter God's unseen kingdom. God has fulfilled all necessary prophecies and removed spiritual obstacles to our entrance into His Kingdom. Those who suggest otherwise interpret the Bible through separation rather than the Oneness of the resurrected Christ.

The current Bible reflects humanity's feeble attempt to recreate the Ark of the Covenant for religious purposes. Just as Israel carried God in a wooden box through the desert, today's Bible serves a similar purpose. We were created to be God's living Ark by establishing an eternal covenant with the resurrected Christ.

■ THE ORIGIN OF TODAY'S BIBLE

For those unfamiliar with its origin, I included an article by Mallory Challis outlining the process.

Oral tradition

It is often assumed by scholars that oral tradition among early Israelite communities is where the contents of the Bible originated. This, of course, cannot be proved with documented manuscripts, so it is difficult to point to a specific date or year when the stories found in the Hebrew Bible, what Christians call the "Old Testament," began to exist.

Original Manuscripts: Hebrew Bible

There has been debate about when the Hebrew Bible began to be written down, but the oldest possible manuscripts of a biblical text archaeologists have found are the Ketef Hinnom Scrolls, which were written in the seventh century BCE.

They read in Hebrew, "May Yahweh bless you and keep you; May Yahweh cause his face to Shine upon you and grant you Peace." This is similar to Numbers 6:24-26.

It is possible that Hebrew literature existed in some form well before 700 BCE, but we do not have those physical documents. The earliest copies of parts of the Hebrew Bible are from *the Dead Sea Scrolls,* a set of texts found in the Qumran caves and that include both biblical and non-biblical manuscripts. These can be dated between the third and first centuries BCE.

The Masoretic Text, produced in the 10th century CE (Common Era), was the first complete manuscript of the Hebrew Bible. This text is still used in synagogues today and is the complete Hebrew manuscript on which all modern English translations of the Old Testament are based.

The first ever known Bible translation is the Septuagint, the first Greek translation of Hebrew Scriptures. The Septuagint was created for Greek-speaking Jews and included books Jews eventually decided weren't authoritative.

But Christians at the time accepted these books as having some kind of authority, even though eventually Christians would come to disagree about this. These texts are the Apocrypha, scripture for Catholics and Orthodox, not for Protestants.

The New Testament texts are easier to trace since these letters and narratives were better preserved by early Christians. Although there are debates on the exact dating of each New Testament book, it is agreed that all the books found in the canonized New Testament were written between 48 and 125 CE.

The first unified collection of New Testament books came about in the late fourth century CE: *the Codex Sinaiticus*. Curators of a preservation project describe the Codex Sinaiticus as "one of the most important books in the world. Handwritten well over 1,600 years ago, the manuscript contains the Christian Bible in Greek, including the oldest complete copy of the New Testament. Its **heavily corrected text** is of outstanding importance for the history of the Bible and the manuscript — the oldest substantial book to survive Antiquity — is of supreme importance for the history of the book."

The Thirty-Ninth Festal Letter

It was not until the late fourth century that the collection of books in the New Testament were first recognized as "canonical" alongside the Hebrew Bible.

In 367 CE, the church father Athanasius wrote his Thirty-Ninth Festal Letter, in which he acknowledged what is called the "closed canon" of the Bible.

Although disputed by others, his letter ultimately mirrored what would become canonical in the New Testament, drawing a sharp line between the texts he saw fit for ecclesiastical use, and those texts he thought were heretical and therefore considered "Apocrypha."

This letter was a response to the battles against heresy early church fathers were experiencing at the time.

Athanasius wanted to protect Christian orthodoxy from *Arianism*, the non-trinitarian heresy that Jesus was not God, but a creature made by God, and thus subordinate to God the Father.

Athanasius provided the basis for the biblical canon, although conversations on what books should be considered "canonical" continued for quite some time.

It was not until April 1546 during the Council of Trent that the Latin Vulgate translation was affirmed as the authoritative version of Scripture. And thus, the Bible as we know it was born.

***The Latin Vulgate* was translated by St. Jerome in 382 CE. This was the first complete Latin version of the entire Old and New Testaments plus the Apocrypha, translated for use in the Latin-speaking church at the time.**

Although there were other Latin versions of the Bible before this, the Vulgate standardized them. Additionally, different versions of the Vulgate have existed throughout church history, such as the Gutenberg Bible published in the 1450s but not used by many Christians today.

***William Tyndale's New Testament* became the first printed part of the Protestant Bible translated directly from Hebrew and Greek.**

At the time, it was illegal to translate the Bible into a vernacular language, although Tyndale did so anyway to make the Bible more accessible for reading. Because of this, he was executed by the Catholic Church in 1536, prior to the completion of his Bible translation.

Miles Coverdale completed the translation for him, finishing the first ever complete translation of the Bible in English.

Later, the Douai-Rheims Bible was translated, not from the original Hebrew and Greek manuscripts, but from the Latin Vulgate into English, published in two different parts.

The New Testament was published in 1582, and the Old Testament was published 30 years later between 1609-1610.

The Douai-Rheims Bible was the standard Bible for English-speaking Catholics until the 1960s, and because it is intended for use in the Catholic Church, it includes some texts that do not appear in Protestant Bibles.

These historical Bible translations set the stage for modern translations that are recognizable to Christians today. Now, all modern English translations of the Bible are based on the Hebrew and Greek texts, not translated through Latin.

Thus, from oral tradition through Hebrew, Greek, Latin and English, the collection of books we now call the "Bible" has quite a long history.[2]

---

[2] https://baptistnews.com/article/crash-course-in-bible-history-how-the-bible-came-to-be/

The Greek term for the Bible is actually 'scrolls', which gives us insight into man's hand in creating the Bible. The Bible as we know it today represents, at most, a mere fractional insight into the vastness of God's Spirit and wisdom.

Additionally, the true essence of the Bible is felt through the unseen exchanges that occur within a person's soul during interactions with our Creator. These experiences transcend mere words on a page or interpretations and are part of what motivates you to read this book.

Since God lives within us as the Holy Spirit, we can seek truth free from historical influences, current situations, or skewed interpretations of scripture. **This strengthens my conviction that once we establish a living covenant with the risen Christ, we become the living New Testament**.

This book, called the Bible, is a key to understanding profound mysteries in His creation through the Holy Spirit. Our challenge in uncovering these truths lies in language and conditioning. This book is written to provide revelation and information for a deeper understanding of God's kingdom's.

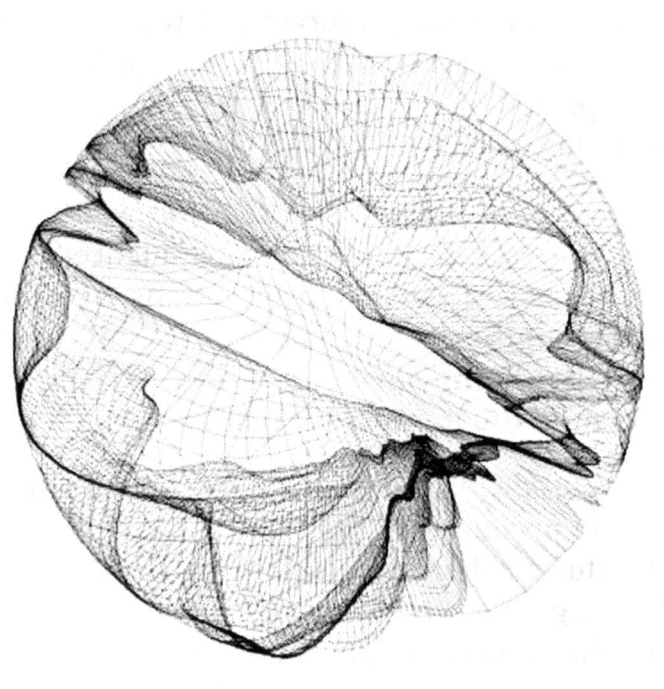

CHAPTER 13

COVENANTS

We have arrived at the heart of our quest to uncover what hinders our longing for liberation from the challenges surrounding us. The echoes of death and destruction continually torment the inhabitants of this planet. Uncovering this essential truth will offer a freedom that will propel your transformation and, what's more, open heaven over your lives.

Our journey to discover His remarkable treasures leads us to one of God's amazing creations: covenants. Adam's failure led God to implement a spiritual ladder to restore unity with His creation. Adam's disobedience allowed the anti-Christ spirit, known as satan, to become the ruler of Earth and the second heaven, influencing humanity's thoughts.

One might wonder why God didn't simply banish satan and start anew. The answer lies in God's righteousness, which compels Him to honor the spiritual laws He established. He allows creation the freedom to choose and respects those decisions, embodying true righteousness.

Therefore, God selected certain individuals at appointed times to form covenants that represented the spiritual achievements made before time. Each of these covenants served as a temporary sign, anticipating the resurrection of His Son, who would inhabit all those who were in Him prior to the creation of the world.

Do you see the beauty of this? We were in Him before the foundation of the world but now He is in us and we are in Him. Does this remind you of a verse in John?

> **"In a little while the world will no longer see Me, but you will see Me.** You will live because I live.
>
> **On that day you will know** that I am in My Father and that you are in Me and that I am in you."
>
> John 14:19-20 GW

Jesus is explaining to His disciples that His physical presence is coming to an end because He has completed His assignment. Nevertheless, He is pulling back the curtain for all those in Him before the world to see Him and His Father as One. That Day is the moment you see His kingdom, as He explained to Nicodemus in John 3. That day is available now, not just after you die physically.

The covenant we reestablish with Christ occurred before our first breath; however, conditioning in this dimension has erased our memories and dulled our frequencies. Be encouraged, for you are recalling your future as you read.

▪ HEAVEN'S BETRAYAL REPRODUCED ON EARTH

The Bible presents several covenants, but this discussion focuses on God's agreements with five specific men. These were key to allowing His Son to fulfill the divine plan for humanity's salvation and enabling individuals to form a personal covenant with Him spiritually.

Adam's betrayal seemed to underscore a profound failure on God's part, resulting in a flooded earth and the death of all humanity except Noah and his family. Nevertheless, this event paved the way for His grand design, which would forever establish His Kingdom on earth and confirm His authority in heaven.

The prophets Isaiah and Ezekiel portray a celestial scene in which Lucifer leads a rebellion in heaven to overthrow God. His betrayal persuaded millions of angels to attempt a coup that mirrored what would happen on earth. His failure, along with Judas's betrayal, brought eternal death to both figures.

The prophets depicted events in heaven that led God to hide His divine plan from the angels. This plan was intended to remove those who opposed Him both on earth and in heaven. God's final Adam accomplished the restoration of His kingdom on earth, reflecting its heavenly form.

The heavenly events represented in the scriptures below served as the unseen backdrop on earth, culminating in Judas's betrayal and crucifixion of Jesus:

> *How you are fallen from heaven, daystar, son of the morning! How you are cut down to the ground, who laid the nations low!*
>
> *You said in your heart, I will ascend into heaven, I will exalt my throne above the stars of God; and I will sit on the mountain of congregation, in the uttermost parts of the north. I will ascend above the heights of the clouds; I will make myself like the Most High.*
>
> *Yet you shall be brought down to Sheol, to the uttermost parts of the pit.*
>
> Isaiah 14:12-15 WEB

> *You were the anointed cherub who covers. Then I set you up on the holy mountain of God. You have walked up and down in the middle of the stones of fire.*
>
> *You were perfect in your ways from the day that you were created, until unrighteousness was found in you.*
>
> Ezekiel 28:14-15 WEB

The splendid design of our Creator reflects an infinite love. This scripture, often quoted yet frequently misunderstood, encapsulates that love:

> *"For God loved the world so much that He gave His only Son, so that everyone who believes in Him may not die but have eternal life."*
>
> John 3:16

The key element of this scripture becomes evident when we substitute "world" with "consciousness," emphasizing the mindset each individual inherits at birth. Jesus, the Godman, willingly became the sacrificial lamb for humanity's sin consciousness, which originated with Adam's betrayal.

This represents a divine love that transcends human understanding. This is why Jesus began His teachings on the kingdom with a call for repentance, encouraging us to alter our mindset. Our thoughts are corrupted from generations of doubt and unbelief, shaped by satan's pollution from the second heaven before his expulsion.

Love is a remarkable power that goes beyond our world and embodies the essence of God. The covenant of salvation began with Israel through the Law, which was temporary until Jesus was sacrificed for all of creation.

Love is the fruit of faith, working in conjunction with righteousness, which is established through covenants—the method our Creator and King uses to ensure the visible reflects the invisible.

God made a covenant with each individual in this section as a prophetic image of His Son's victorious redemption and kingdom, which was completed before time began. This is an essential key for each of us to remember. Our redemption was purchased before our physical manifestation because we were in Him before there was time.

I have come to understand that salvation is a transformative covenant made possible by the cross of Jesus, granting eternal life to all who call upon His name, no matter their circumstances or mindset. Yet, this represents only a fraction of what Jesus achieved after His resurrection.

I believe Jesus returned the kingdom to His Father at the same time that God entrusted this world to Jesus, as depicted in the book of Corinthians, which we will explore in depth in the following section.

> *Then comes the end, when He hands over the kingdom to God the Father, when He has brought to an end all rule and all authority and power.*
>
> *The last enemy to be eliminated is death.*
>
> 1 Corinthians 15:24, 26 NET

Numerous people find it difficult to understand this scripture, having been misled into thinking that Jesus will return and that we are still subject to physical death. These misunderstandings arise from a mindset that emphasizes our physical existence rather than acknowledging our spiritual essence.

To truly appreciate God's royalty and wisdom, we begin by exploring His first covenant. As we open our hearts to the different covenants, we'll find that His ways deepen our understanding, helping it to expand in wonderful ways beyond what we currently know.

■ TEMPORARY COVENANTS

A. NOAH

We begin with Noah to examine the covenants and observe the magnificence of God's divine plan. The devastating flood that wiped out all life, except for

Noah and his family, occurred due to Lucifer's pride and the involvement of angels with the inhabitants of earth.

Keep in mind that the chaos in heaven caused by Lucifer's rebellion was reflected on earth as well. Adam's betrayal ensured that sin would spread through all generations, necessitating the arrival of the "last Adam" to fulfill what the first Adam could not achieve.

Nevertheless, Adam's sin consciousness is present in the blood of every person born into this realm. The refusal to accept this is why science will continue wandering in the desert, like the early Israelites attempting to discover the "secret of life" that will validate their unbelief in God.

You might wonder: Wasn't God always able to save His fallen creation? While He had the capability, He recognized that altering the outcome of our free will would undermine faith, which is the source of His love and the foundation of His being.

Noah served as the vessel for God's initial covenant, which was intended for both the planet and himself. God's grand design demanded a universe and a planet in harmonious order. The covenant with Noah, marked by a rainbow, guaranteed the safety and redemption of the "earth" and the universe within this dimension.

> *The odor of the sacrifice pleased the LORD, and he said to himself, Never again will I put the earth under a curse*

because of what people do; I know that from the time they are young their thoughts are evil. **Never again will I destroy all living beings, as I have done this time.**

Genesis 8:21 TEV

"When the rainbow appears in the clouds, I will see it and **remember the everlasting covenant between me and all living beings on earth.**

That is the sign of the promise which I am making to all living beings."

Genesis 9:16–17 TEV

I have come across interpretations referencing Peter's letter, which mentions a divine fire meant to devastate the earth. This serves as yet another instance of the ignorant mindset that contributed to the formation of today's Bible. God's covenants are intended to bring His creation together, rather than the human-made religions and Bibles that aim to divide us.

Humans became aware of the rainbow after losing their spiritual bandwidth as Godmen. In simpler terms, this loss signified giving up their higher status in the second heaven, along with the vibrational frequencies of that dimension.

The more we focus on the material world, the denser our vibrational wavelength becomes. As a result, a slower vibration draws our attention more towards the material realm and the shadows created by the fourth day's lights in this realm.

Before humanity lost its spiritual authority, we resonated at a higher frequency, like the light of the first day in Genesis 1. This light was colorless; losing that frequency allows us to see colors, which, while beautiful, signifies our separation from Oneness.

B. ABRAHAM

Abraham exemplifies the quintessential model of faith through which God disseminated His love across the earth. It is my belief that God recalled Abraham each time Israel forsook Him in favor of idols. The longsuffering of God is, and has always been, a direct consequence of this dynamic covenant, as He was aware that His lineage would serve as the bloodline for Jesus.

God's covenant with Abraham exemplifies God's nature, particularly when considering Abraham's willingness to sacrifice Isaac, his only son. This moment foreshadows Jesus' sacrifice, which God ultimately spared Abraham from. Nevertheless, it represents a faith that was recognized as righteousness, capturing the essence that underpins all covenants.

> *When God made His promise to Abraham, He made a vow to do what He had promised. Since there was no one greater than Himself, He used His own name when He made His vow.*
>
> Hebrews 6:13 TEV

God formed a distinct covenant with Himself to maintain the integrity and righteousness of Abraham's faith. Furthermore, this covenant mirrors the one Jesus embodies at the cross for all humanity who call upon His Name.

> **I make this covenant with you:** *I promise that you will be the ancestor of many nations.*
>
> *I will keep my promise to you and to your descendants in future generations as an everlasting covenant. I will be your God and the God of your descendants.*
>
> Genesis 17:4,7 TEV

Many of Abraham's descendants became instruments of satan during Jesus' crucifixion because of their access to worldly riches, referred to by Jesus as Mammon. While this choice offered wealth and fame, it also led to persecution and suffering. The anti-Christ spirit represents those who think that this worldly system can offer the security they desire, without being in covenant with Christ.

Nevertheless, God's covenant with Abraham established a blessed people who would both steward and reap the fruits of the land. One of the most significant aspects of this covenant was Abraham's introduction to Melchizedek.

Adam was meant to be the steward and high priest of the earth, but his lack of faith corrupted both humanity and the land. Consequently, after the earth's fall, God sought a priest to serve humanity and the land. This priest was Melchizedek, who reconnected heaven and earth through his worship.

C. MELCHIZEDEK

I am including Melchizedek in the section regarding the temporary covenant due to his relationship with Abraham. We become part of the priesthood under the Melchizedek Order immediately upon entering into a covenant with the risen Christ. Jesus, as the last Adam, served as God's steward and priest on earth, and that divine assignment is bestowed upon us in Christ.

God beautifully introduced His spiritual priesthood through Melchizedek, especially since the law of Moses appointed the tribe of Levites as priests. This was part of a perfect plan, as this tribe was linked to Caiaphas and Annas, the high priests who played a significant role in the crucifixion of Christ.

The covenant with Abraham served as the cornerstone of God's master plan, restoring righteousness on earth through the faith of both Melchizedek and Abraham. Every subsequent covenant expanded upon the foundation laid by this blood oath.

God made a covenant with the planet through Noah, and His covenant with Abraham established the bloodline for His Son to restore His Kingdom. However, He needed a priesthood that could minister to Him on behalf of His creation.

> *Abraham gave Melchizedek a tenth of everything he had captured. (a)*
>
> *No one knows anything about Melchizedek's father, mother, or ancestors. No one knows when he was born or when he died. Like the Son of God, Melchizedek continues to be a priest forever.*
>
> *You can see how important Melchizedek was. Abraham gave him a tenth of what he had captured, even though Abraham was the father of the chosen people.*
>
> Hebrews 7:2(a)-4 GWT

God was orchestrating a series of events on Earth that necessitated a lasting spiritual priesthood, unlike the temporary Levitical priesthood. Melchizedek represented this enduring priesthood and, akin to the "Son of God," foreshadowed God's royal priest, Christ. This priesthood consistently offers worship to God as a result of the resurrection.

Melchizedek serves as a reminder that the priests of God worship Him in spirit and truth. This aspect constitutes the prerequisite that God seeks in His worshippers, for this form of worship facilitates the earth's provision for God's priests.

We acknowledge the covenant of bread and wine that Abraham formed with Melchizedek, but do we fully grasp that this represented a covenant with the earth and all material things? Essentially, God was affirming to Abraham that the earth would generously meet all the material needs of his descendants.

Melchizedek symbolizes God's eternal priesthood for all of creation, both seen and unseen. The Melchizedek priesthood is often misunderstood, as it represents the spiritual priesthood through which Christ ministers eternally.

When we enter into a covenant with the risen Christ, we might forget that He and His priesthood reside within us. Do you truly grasp this? We frequently call ourselves the "church," but it becomes more evident when you understand that the risen Christ, in the form of Melchizedek, lives within you. We embody both the physical and spiritual dimensions of creation, as the living source of all that is seen and unseen dwells within us.

The tangible Melchizedek roamed the earth devoid of history or lineage, representing individuals outside time and space, existing in Christ before the foundation of the world. We serve, conscious of our roots beyond this constrained realm, liberated from death and fear.

God foresaw the corruption of the Levitical Priesthood, recognizing it as a temporary remedy for salvation until Christ could dwell within those who remember they were in Him before the world's foundation.

The next key figure in His plan was Moses, whom Pharaoh raised. A monumental battle between good and evil was about to unfold in Egypt. Interestingly, it was Abraham's great-great-nephew Joseph who saved the nation, setting the stage for this confrontation.

D. MOSES

More than a thousand years after Abraham's death, his descendants, known as the Hebrews, became slaves in Egypt. In a remarkable continuation of His promise, God upheld His covenant with Abraham by forming a new covenant with Moses, thus guaranteeing the fulfillment of Abraham's wish for the liberation of his cherished descendants.

> **"Now, if you will obey Me and keep My covenant,** *you will be My own people. The whole earth is Mine, but you will be My chosen people,"*
> Exodus 19:5 TEV

God's covenant with Moses marked the beginning of a temporary collective covenant with Abraham's descendants, established through His Law and the Levitical priesthood. The Mosaic Law and the Ten Commandments form the cornerstone of society's concepts of good and evil, serving as a foundation for our judicial system. Moreover, just as in the days of Jesus, they have become the model adopted by religions around the world.

> **For the law, having a shadow** of the good things to come, and not the very image of the things, can never with these same sacrifices, which they offer continually year by year, make those who approach perfect.
>
> Hebrews 10:1 NKJ

This temporary covenant provided salvation to everyone who adhered to the instructions given to Moses. However, as mentioned in Hebrews, it was only a shadow of the true Light, which manifested as Jesus.

However, the churches today exhibit the same mindset as those in Jesus' time. To accomplish God's design and plans, the Law had to be established until satan's expulsion, similar to Lucifer's banishment from heaven.

Moses, cherished by God, represented the Law that demanded righteousness and imposed consequences for disobedience. Consequently, he could not cross the Jordan River due to disobeying God's instruction to speak to the rock for water; he struck it instead. This may seem a severe punishment until one understands the full context.

The Law was a temporary covenant established through Moses to fulfill God's prophecy in Genesis, where He told the serpent (paraphrasing) that someone would crush your head, though you will bruise his heel. God would sacrifice His Son to eliminate the accuser who used the Law to condemn creation.

> *Now there was a day when the sons of God came to present themselves before the LORD, and Satan also came among them.*
>
> Job 1:6 NKJ

> *In another vision the LORD showed me the High Priest Joshua standing before the angel of the LORD. And there beside Joshua stood Satan, ready to bring an accusation against him.*
>
> *The angel of the LORD said to Satan, "May the LORD condemn you, Satan! May the LORD, who loves Jerusalem, condemn you. This man is like a stick snatched from the fire."*
>
> Zechariah 3:1-2 TEV

> *Then I heard a loud voice speaking in Heaven. It said, The salvation and the power and the Kingdom of our God have now come, and the sovereignty of His Christ; for the accuser of our brethren has been hurled down—he who, day after day and night after night, was wont to accuse them in the presence of God.*
>
> Revelation 12:10

The law explicitly mandates the execution of anyone who kills an innocent person. Thus, God justly eliminated satan using the very law that accused those redeemed by His blood. Unfortunately, collateral damage also fell upon Moses, who defied God's command.

Please understand that the same principles hold for those who regard themselves as righteous while judging and condemning those with differing beliefs. This attitude exemplifies the law, and individuals who continue within this framework, either knowingly or unknowingly, will encounter repercussions.

The wonder of how God created His covenants with individuals and expanded them into a nation is truly extraordinary. I believe the ultimate goal is for us to find rest, just as God did on the seventh day in Genesis. Our ability to establish a covenant with the resurrected Christ ensures that we accomplish our mission.

When we focus only on the cross, we find ourselves connecting our lives with the Babylonian system that Jesus of Nazareth came to dismantle. Putting too much emphasis on salvation can feel like the Law of Moses, implying that we should just sit back and wait for our Messiah to save us from this world. It's crucial for us to shift our mindset, as Jesus taught us, so we can embrace His kingdom and steer clear of this trap.

Nevertheless, if focusing on the cross and reaffirming your covenant with Jesus of Nazareth brings you peace, then that's absolutely wonderful! I truly believe everyone has their own path, and I'm simply here to share my experiences with you.

During the Transfiguration of Jesus, Moses was granted a vision of the promised land, which he was unable to enter physically. This underscores the reality of the invisible realm and cautions that an exclusive focus on the physical world diminishes the spiritual strength needed for transformation.

One of the most important outcomes of God's law is that it reveals the anti-Christ spirit. The law is the fuel that produces the anti-Christ spirit, which is the same today as it was during the time of Jesus. This reminds us that God's physical covenants were a temporary safeguard for His divine plan on earth and in the heavens.

God required a worship warrior to fulfill His ultimate purpose prior to the advent of Jesus. His covenant with David is regarded as one of the most powerful declarations on earth, as David's kingdom heralded a millennium of peace that has not been observed since, nor shall it be again.

E. DAVID

No figure within the scriptures exemplifies Jesus more accurately than David. David's profound affection for Jehovah is consistently demonstrated throughout his life and in the Psalms.

> *Keep me as the apple of Your eye;*
> Psalm 17:8 NKJ

The Psalms celebrate David's life as a worshipper and warrior, contributing to God's covenant with him. The same love that led God to sacrifice His Son was shared with David. David's work precedes the spiritual work of His Son.

David overcame the spirit of the anti-Christ represented by the Philistines, paralleling the victory of the resurrected Christ. His accomplishments on Earth mirror Christ's eternal spiritual mission, a connection often overlooked by readers of scripture who focus solely on the physical realm.

> **I have been with you wherever you have gone and have destroyed all the enemies in your path. I shall bring you fame like the fame of the great ones of the earth.**
> 1 Chronicles 17:8 NKJ

Additionally, David's physical throne and authority symbolize what Christ provides to His followers today. Once we enter into a covenant with Christ, we must embrace our role as heirs to His kingdom in both spiritual and physical domains. This signifies that we become kings and priests like Melchizedek, placing all our enemies beneath us.

In Psalms 22, God enlightens David to the horrible pain of Jesus on the cross, allowing him to understand his spiritual connection with the one who would come through his bloodline:

> *My God, my God,*
> *why have you abandoned me*
>
> *Why are you so far from my deliverance*
> *and from my words of groaning*
>
> *My God, I cry by day,*
> *but you do not answer,*
> *by night, yet I have no rest.*
>
> Psalm 22:1-2 CSB

This shows that our covenant with Christ truly enriches our ability to receive revelations that go beyond time and space. Unlike David, Christ has finished His work, allowing our prophetic insight to reflect what has already been achieved. This transforms any fear of impending doom into the uplifting joy of being seated with Him in His kingdom.

> **Your house and your kingdom shall be made sure for ever before you: your throne shall be established forever.**
>
> 2 Samuel 7:16 WEB

This scripture has been fulfilled; however, due to our belief that Jesus must physically occupy a throne in Jerusalem, many overlook its perfection. It is important to read this scripture in the Book of Revelation while bearing in mind that the arrangement of this book was conducted by man rather than the Holy Spirit.

> *I saw an angel coming down from heaven, holding the key to the bottomless pit and a large chain in his hand.*
>
> *He overpowered the serpent, that ancient snake, named Devil and Satan. The angel chained up the serpent for 1,000 years.*
>
> Revelation 20:1-2 WEY

The reality is that God's covenant with David initiated a millennium of peace and prosperity across the globe. Although this period may have physically concluded, it commenced spiritually with the birth of Jesus.

The unfortunate truth is those who created the Bible, whether out of ignorance or malice, interpreted the book of Revelation as a future event.

Satan was chained and confined for a millennium, unaware that the "headcrusher" would manifest on the very day of his release. The throne of David became the spiritual kingdom of God for all those with understanding.

This image illustrates the transformation from physical to spiritual in God's covenants and shows why the Bible should not be fragmented. Dividing it leads to chaos and division.

Every servant of God accomplished their missions through these temporary covenants, paving the way for a glorious ascension into God's kingdom and our rightful reign with Christ. This remarkable plan is fulfilled in Christ. Religion cannot grasp God's ways, as its authority isn't divinely ordained. Jesus emphasized that earthly existence offers no spiritual profit.

This covenant is the final part of history's remarkable redemptive plan, establishing His kingdom and removing all adversaries. God fulfills *the Genesis 3 promise* majestically, leading all angels to eternally glorify His name before His Throne.

ETERNAL COVENANTS

A. NAME ABOVE ALL NAMES IS SALVATION

Neither humanity nor a temple can establish a kingdom of righteousness on earth. This is why Jesus was born. His physical body became God's instrument for a spiritual kingdom. The main challenge for Jesus' followers is recognizing the power of understanding ourselves as spirit and consciously observing our tendency to remain separate from oneness.

David's covenant served as a physical manifestation of God's unwavering faithfulness in honoring His commitments to all individuals who enter into a covenant with Him. However, God declined David's request to construct a house or temple in His honor. The temple contributed to Israel's downfall and the crucifixion of Jesus, resulting in God distancing David from that calamity.

> *Jesus said to them, "You're from below. I'm from above. You're from this world. I'm not from this world."*
>
> John 8:23 GWT

In essence, He was a Godman infused with His Father's blood, indicating that His thoughts and imaginations differed from those of humanity. His earthly existence was to accomplish God's divine plan of making a covenant with each of us.

Before the crucifixion, Jesus drank from the cup of wine, symbolizing His heavenly blood in exchange for the blood of Adam and all his descendants. This covenant represents His agreement with His Father to endure the terrible physical death and subsequent descent into hell.

The cross at Golgatha represented a grim destiny set even before the world's inception, fulfilling God's prophecy in Genesis. No other death on earth can match this Roman brutality, which we are encouraged to remember whenever we face the fear of death.

This profound sacrifice frees humanity from the debt incurred by Adam's transgression and becomes the replacement for the salvation offered only to Israel through the Law.

Jesus fulfilled the Old Covenant and established the covenant of salvation for all who believe in His sacrifice and call upon His name as Joel and Paul write in the following verses:

> *Then whoever calls on the name of the LORD will be saved.*
>
> Joel 2:32 NKJ

> *So then, "Whoever calls on the name of the Lord will be saved."*
>
> Romans 10:13 GWT

Paul indicates in the Book of Acts that his calling was to proclaim grace, which constitutes the essence of salvation.

> *but I make account of none of these, neither do I count my life precious to **myself, so that I finish my course with joy, and the ministration that I received** from the Lord Jesus, to testify fully the good news of the grace of God.*
>
> Acts 20:24 YLT

Salvation is the victory we enjoy from Jesus' death on the cross, fulfilling the law and God's promise to satan in the Garden. However, it does not reveal the invisible kingdom of God restored at Christ's resurrection. Jesus tells Nicodemus we will see the invisible kingdom, which I have never experienced through salvation.

> *Jesus said to him, "Truly, I say to you, **Without a new birth no man is able to see the kingdom of God.**"*
>
> John 3:3 BBE

Nonetheless, it offers important insights into why modern churches prioritize the message of salvation. This reasoning is based on the belief that the Bible is correctly divided into the Old and New Testaments. As a result, there is a belief that Paul's teachings are relevant to every generation starting from 2000 years ago.

Many Christians today perceive salvation as a gift from Jesus, achieved by reciting verses from Romans and undergoing water baptism. They correctly believe that calling upon Jesus's name establishes a covenant with Him, Jesus of Nazareth.

Only after entering into a covenant with the risen Christ, signifying a "new birth," did my spiritual vision awaken to recognize what exists beyond the physical realm. Gaining this understanding has taken nearly 50 years, yet it is indeed a remarkable experience.

Furthermore, the discerning individual would comprehend that the Bible achieved its completion on the day of Christ's resurrection, as this event represented the fulfillment of God's original prophecy outlined in Genesis. God conveyed to the devil that his reign would be temporary, as He intended to send One to ultimately defeat him. (paraphrased)

> "On that day you will know that I am in My Father and that you are in Me and that I am in you."
>
> John 14:20 NKJ

What day is Jesus referring to? I believe it is the day we are spiritually reunited with our origin in Him. For me, this began when I transcended my covenant of salvation and dared to believe I could spiritually covenant with the resurrected Christ. This journey has neither a beginning nor an end, which I now see as the seventh day that God chose as His resting place.

B. CHRIST THE NEW TESTAMENT

For those convinced that Jesus and Christ are identical and that distinct covenants don't matter, I share that this was my belief for many years until I genuinely sought guidance from the Holy Spirit. I can't say whether His responses come to you as they do to me, but for me, His replies are never straightforward yes or no. Rather, He communicates with me through unexpected experiences.

For instance, I requested Him to clarify the concept of "new birth" as though I were Nicodemus. Unexpectedly, I started recognizing aspects of quantum physics—details I had previously missed. This not only piqued my interest but also allowed me to grasp the ideas. My comprehension has grown considerably beyond my initial capabilities and interests, and it is still evolving.

This process inspired me to write the series "ever ascending" because our spiritual connection to Him is profoundly deep—there's nothing in this dimension we have not contributed to or comprehended. NOTHING. This is why we are not separate from what our senses define, and maintaining that perspective limits our ability to transcend the mindset of this realm.

The final covenant of God serves as the beautiful model He used with Abraham to establish a bloodline for Jesus. He embodies us, ensuring that our covenant with Christ brings us back to our origin and provides us with abundance throughout our time in a physical body.

> *Blessed be the God and Father of our Lord Jesus Christ, who has crowned us with every spiritual blessing in the heavenly realms in Christ.*
>
> *even as, in His love,* ***He chose us as His own in Christ before the creation of the world,*** *that we might be holy and without blemish in His presence.*
>
> Ephesians 1:3-4 WEY

The Bible beautifully shows how God fulfills His promises from Genesis to Revelation. If your life isn't aligning with your expectations as a believer, it might be worth considering whether your focus is truly on a relationship with Christ or more on the letters of Paul, Peter, and John. These inspiring men experienced incredible testimonies and revelations because they had a genuine and vibrant covenant with the resurrected Christ.

Recall that Jesus expressed, "*I have given them My glory,*" referring to His apostles. This represents the power over death and the fear associated with it. In my view, His glory is equivalent to receiving the covenant that He and His Father established before the foundation of the world.

All of the apostles made covenants with the risen Christ, but their covenant was never meant to substitute for our personal covenant with Him. The Kingdom of God is His dwelling place, and our access is directly proportionate to our knowledge of the resurrected Christ. That is what He meant in the following scripture:

> *"Don't let your heart be troubled. Believe in God. Believe also in Me.*
>
> *In My Father's house are many mansions. If it weren't so, I would have told you. I am going to prepare a place for you.*
>
> *If I go and prepare a place for you, I will come again and will receive you to Myself; that where I am, you may be there also.*
>
> *Where I go, you know, and you know the way."*
>
> John 14:1-4 WEB

Jesus completed His earthly mission and was departing to embody the kingdom, returning as The Spirit for all humanity to establish a covenant with His resurrected essence, which can be seen in a new birth. He welcomed them before their physical deaths, which explains why they accomplished greater works.

CHAPTER 13 | COVENANTS

The goal of making a covenant with Christ is for people to represent the New Testament on earth, receiving ever-increasing revelations to share with future generations. Each generation must not limit itself to previous revelations of Christ, or it will become another religion.

The New Covenant of Christ continuously grows and resonates with the dynamic frequencies of the Father, whose commitment to grant us His kingdom demands expansion to fulfill His divine purposes.

The infinite power and grandeur of the divine continually transcend time and space, yet religion consistently rejects what it cannot govern. As a result, it cultivates a mindset in individuals that positions them as victims dependent on Christ for transformation. This represents the anti-Christ spirit we previously addressed, whose influences shape the laws, governments, education, and communication within our societal systems.

Those wishing to establish a personal covenant with Christ will find inspiration and fulfill this incredible commitment. No menu or physical action is needed other than the desire to be One with Him, as you were before becoming flesh. This conscious choice allows the Holy Spirit access and offers additional revelations on your journey back to your origin.

We understand that we need to change our thinking to expand our mental bandwidth, but how often do we recognize when our comfort with the familiar hinders our progress? This highlights the importance of being aware in each moment.

We must avoid complicating our relationship with the King of Kings by blending past beliefs with the covenant made with the risen Christ. This highlights the necessity of staying focused on the present, as there are no past errors to grapple with; the present is eternal.

See your life as His completed work from within; this perspective will transform your life experience. Moreover, it will boost your confidence in the unknown and encourage boldness in your endeavors.

The following chapters aim to transform how we pray and believe. They remind you of what you already know but may have forgotten due to complacency. Staying conscious helps break habits, allowing greater reliance on the Holy Spirit.

CHAPTER 13 — COVENANTS

FAITH AND BELIEVE

We have arrived at the section of the book that offers both practical and spiritual advice, which has guided me in my unwavering pursuit of His kingdom for many years.

However, it is crucial to recognize that there is no ultimate destination, as we have always existed. We have been conditioned to believe that this limited dimension and its illusions are reality.

Faith serves as both the origin and the culmination of love. Thus, those who embrace God's love place their trust in Him. Faith cannot exist without love; individuals attempting to pray without love or gratitude for their present circumstances are out of tune with God's essence. We will explore this further in the chapter dedicated to prayer.

The present moment is the home of faith, as it possesses neither past nor future; in truth, it does not exist within this limited dimension. Remember, all material things originated from the invisible realm. Thus, faith is the foundation of everything, both seen and unseen from God who is in essence love.

One observation that aids in establishing our trust in the unknown is how we use the terms faith and believe. Faith and believe should be regarded as one, just as Christ and His word are united, reflecting the oneness of His soul, mind, and spirit.

> *"That's why I tell you to **have faith** that you have already received whatever you pray for, and it will be yours."*
>
> Mark 11:24 GWT

> *"That is why I tell you, as to whatever you pray and make request for, **if you believe** that you have received it it shall be yours."*
>
> Mark 11:24 WEY

The mind of Christ is submitted to His spirit, which is why He could eloquently describe the symbiotic relationship between the words "believe" and "faith" in this verse. Using the word "faith" in place of "believe" in your daily conversations will make you aware of where your trust lies.

How many times have we prayed for something that did not materialize? A significant revelation that helped me understand this was recognizing my own doubt.

I often used "believe" to express my lukewarm endorsement of a situation. For example, when my employer asked if I believed my coworker could fulfill a task, I said yes. However, I had reservations due to his past performance.

In other words, I did not have faith or total assurance in their (his) ability, so I half-heartedly replied accordingly. The term "believe" finds its origin within the physical realm, as humanity exists in a state of separation from God from the moment of birth.

After you discover the truth is inside us from birth, your hearts and minds will be one, and you will stop looking outside yourself for confirmation of what you already have.

On the other hand, the term "faith" relates to spirituality, denoting a harmony between the heart and mind. This understanding led to a profound transformation in my life, and I believe yours can undergo a similar change as well.

Abraham was well-known for using the word "believe" to express his faith in God. I argue that this is why God could trust him with the covenant. Abraham recognized God's Christ because of his faith in God, and this belief transformed into the faith that God needed to fulfill His plan.

> *"Your father Abraham was overjoyed to see My day; he saw it and was glad."*
>
> John 8:56 NKJ

To connect the invisible to the visible, we must become what we pray. According to Mark 11, you need to believe that what you are asking God for already exists.

In essence, we usually hear thunder following the sight of lightning, as light moves faster than sound in our reality. But what pertains to the spiritual realm? Here, the visible intersects with the invisible in our conscious awareness, which the Bible refers to as faith.

In other words, as spiritual beings, nothing is impossible since every potential outcome resides within us. I have discovered that my mental separation from my heart created the opposition that Abraham did not experience, as he expressed being "glad" as if he were already feeling it.

This transformation did not occur overnight; however, the longer I resisted the urge to doubt or to rely on my senses to validate the outcome, the more rapidly it began to manifest.

My belief evolved into faith as my emotional excitement transformed the invisible into the visible.

This emotional energy connected my heart to my mind, allowing me to embody what I believed.

I define faith as knowing without learning. As spirit beings, we are not separate from what God created; that oneness is our origin and destiny.

> *It is by faith that we understand that the universe was created by God's word, so that what can be seen was made out of what cannot be seen.*
>
> Hebrews 11:3 TEV

> *by faith we understand the ages to have been prepared by a saying of God, in regard to the things seen not having come out of things appearing;*
>
> Hebrews 11:3 YLT

We are the creation of God and His Word, which fundamentally connects us to the source of our perceptions.

A. WHOLENESS

Could this explain why Jesus warned against judgment? If we are integral to The Word, then judgment serves one purpose: to heighten our sense of separation from our Creator.

I don't mean to imply that you're an inanimate object; rather, I want you to realize that everything in this realm is made up of energy waves until a conscious observer recognizes their existence through awareness and perception. Our judgments widen the gap by creating the illusion of separation from what we judge, while subtly increasing our dependence on our senses.

Therefore, education in this field could be more impactful by focusing on the interconnectedness through the spiritual dimension, rather than just seeking evidence of our differences.

Humanity has embraced duality, resulting in a profound sense of separation. This decision has fostered an environment of pride, which ultimately leads to self-destruction. It is imperative that we resist influences that are judgmental or divisive.

To recognize the unity in this realm, one just needs to examine the root systems of plants and trees. The interconnectedness of all existence represents heaven on earth and can significantly enhance human communication.

We often focus on matter over spirit, but this can change by being present. In quiet moments, all creation communicates life and unity.

I understand this may sound challenging to those focused on the physical realm, but that perspective fades the longer you stay present. Jesus was and is before all things material, and you and I were in Him before becoming flesh.

We must understand that we are spirit, existing prior to all material things, and this understanding will allow matter to become our servant rather than our master. In other words, if we are in Him before becoming flesh that would make all things part of us, creating no lack or need.

Faith is the invisible consciousness that unveils the truth to those with spiritual eyes and ears.

> *"But blessed are your eyes for they see, and your ears for they hear."*
>
> Matthew 13:16

Today, most people use "believe" to validate what their senses and analytical minds determine as true. Our world is thus defined by our physical senses and brains, programmed across generations in this spacetime dimension. Thinking within these parameters limits our understanding of the truth.

This dimension is created from shadows, making it very easy to disguise the truth. This is why Jesus sent Himself as the Helper. His voice and vibration will break our hypnotic conditioning.

When you focus on the present moment, you'll find it easier to hear Him, and as you stay present longer, His voice will become clearer and more powerful. This beautiful experience will transform from feeling like a burden into a wonderful journey as your life unfolds in extraordinary ways.

B. QUANTUM PRAYER

The essence of faith exists in the present moment, yet most individuals are not truly present while praying. Instead, they often find themselves preoccupied with concerns about past or future events, which motivate their prayers.

Our minds and hearts are designed to align with His, allowing prayer to manifest on earth as it does in heaven. However, our scattered focus hinders our capacity to stay connected long enough to experience the rewards of faith in our prayer practice.

In essence, our prayers resonate at the frequency of our hopes and aspirations, which are generally the result of our current location in time and space. In other words, if we are in the eternal present moment our vibration will represent resurrection not death.

From a young age, we rely on our experiences in the third dimension to affirm our beliefs and shape our identity. Prayer has turned into a means of justifying our separation from God rather than nurturing our connection with Him.

When a person receives a disease diagnosis and requests prayer, our prayer often reinforces that person's disease because we ask God to heal them. Consequently, prayer should focus on thanking God for His divine plan in their life, regardless of physical appearances.

For instance, if someone asked for my prayers after a cancer diagnosis, my first response would be to nonverbally proclaim life rather than death into their unconscious agreement with that declaration.

Praying is not about asking God to do what He has already accomplished, which is the defeat of death; it is, in most cases, an effort to awaken the spiritual being within the physical body that has agreed with such a proclamation.

Ultimately, our spiritual authority must remain unshaken by the physical illusions we accept, as that is not our true identity.

Jesus and His word are one with His Father; consequently, He expresses what He knows. Jesus conveys the spirit, indicating that His words carry His authority and reality from the realm that created all things.

For example, when a physician delivers a prognosis using medical terminology, patients must learn the language of death and repeat it, effectively agreeing with the diagnosis and eventual outcome.

By learning and repeating the words associated with that diagnosis, we resonate with the frequency of death, which aligns with the resonant frequency of our worldly system.

Our language mirrors the frequency of our beliefs and expected outcomes in life. Do we believe that if we pray using the language of this realm, God will be on the same wavelength? The Bible states that faith moves God, which does not conform to the language of this world system.

On the other hand, using Bible verses rarely makes a significant difference because it is not just the words we use but the frequency conveyed in those words. The spirit realm is nonverbal, yet it shapes the material we visualize. Therefore, seeing the whole in every situation alters our perspective and vibration, allowing us to release spiritual words.

For instance, many individuals pray for healing from illness out of fear. They may even refer to the scripture from 1 Peter 2:24 that says, *"by His stripes we are healed."* However, accepting a negative diagnosis from their doctor causes these words to resonate with fear.

The heart is the key in bringing our spoken desires to life by attracting the electrical signals of words and retuning them to the one praying.

Remarkably, the heart's magnetic field quickly responds to the vibrational signature of words that resonate with fear frequencies. This happens because our world operates and is fundamentally based within that same frequency.

Consequently, prayers that reference scripture possess little power if we are resonating with fear, which explains why more individuals perish than survive despite their prayers. We are spiritually created to be united in our thoughts and emotions with Christ.

Picture your thoughts as electrical energy waves sent into the unseen realm. Consider ripples formed when a rock drops into a lake. This analogy represents the electrical signature of thoughts as they emerge in the invisible world.

Imagine these waves as prayers sent from our minds to our understanding of our Heavenly Father. In contrast, the heart discharges magnetic energy waves into the same invisible field, attracting waves that match its waveform. If the heart is fearful, it will magnetically draw waves within that frequency. This illustrates why we attract what we genuinely believe and feel, regardless of what we articulate.

To change this condition, we need to let go of the belief that visible circumstances reflect our spiritual condition. It's clear why we often cling to this idea, but the good news is that we can reverse it by simply choosing to stay present, even when hell is happening all around us.

The human mind and heart actively share and receive waves of energy, beautifully reflecting the divine design set by God for all His creations in this world. Our bodies function as both transmitters and receivers, showcasing the remarkable intention behind God's creation and enabling us to access all the spiritual blessings available to us.

This awareness will significantly aid you in maintaining consciousness, as the Holy Spirit resonates at the perfect frequency to supply everything necessary before you even realize you need it, while also offering you remarkable spiritual energy to enhance your capacity to stay present.

The Holy Spirit transmits and receives signals within the bandwidth of faith, and He is the one who intercedes for those whose minds are stayed on Him.

Changing our resonating frequency is no secret to those who concentrate on the eternal present. Why? Because they have relinquished their belief in this world system as the supreme authority.

My life changed the moment I realized that I am a spirit and that my physical condition is only as real as I perceive it to be. This awareness allowed my spirit to reconnect with its origin.

By remaining aware of the eternal present moment, my thoughts and heart unite as a powerful transmitter, enabling the Holy Spirit to open my eyes and reveal that what I have been asking for was there all along, but my attention was elsewhere.

Our attention span grows in tandem with how fully our minds and hearts engage with the present moment. By nurturing a consistent state of gratitude, no matter the situation we find ourselves in, we amplify our spiritual energy. The union of heaven and earth within us delights God, as He bestows upon us His Kingdom. Through this connection, humanity encounters the diverse beauty of God's creation, which exceeds our wildest imaginations.

New Testament prayer signifies a resurrected life now and beyond, recognizing both material and spiritual aspects within us. Our hesitance to awaken and believe reflects our pride, while recognizing this fosters deep gratitude and love. I share this from personal experience.

The power that awaits our conscious participation in His finished work is unknowable in print, but it is experienced through faith. It has already occurred in time, but you must witness it from your present condition before it changes your perception and understanding.

C. THE FRUIT OF OUR LIPS

> *Through Him then, let us continually offer up a sacrifice of praise to God, that is, the fruit of lips that give thanks to His name.*
>
> Hebrews 13:15 NASB

Through Christ, humanity received an unparalleled gift—so extraordinary that comprehending its entirety will take eternity. However, our limited time on earth allows us to discover the treasures unveiled by His resurrection.

As Jesus conveyed to Nicodemus, the key to discovering these treasures lies in understanding and entering the Kingdom of God, which cannot be accomplished simply by attending church or reciting scripture.

The authority and depth offered through His resurrection to those who seek His kingdom cannot be grasped using worldly wisdom. This is why Jesus began His message with 'repent,' which signifies a transformation in thought. Individuals who acknowledge this and are committed to entering will examine this chapter closely.

The most important feature that will keep you focused and resolute is gratitude. Years ago, I heard the phrase "attitude of gratitude," which sounded cliché until I began this journey.

The profound significance of thanksgiving is neither a cliché nor trivial, as it encapsulates a transformed mindset in individuals who have perceived the incomprehensible completed work of Christ.

The supernatural ability to both reject and relinquish your conditioned self-image within this dimension invigorates your spirit with truth. Furthermore, it enhances all your spiritual senses, granting access to God's multidimensional realms, thereby allowing you to experience freedom like never before.

We have examined the role that experiences play in conditioning our physical bodies. Consequently, it is essential for us to be mindful observers throughout each waking moment of the day, as this enables us to perceive the depth of such conditioning in a nonjudgmental manner. The outcome of this practice alone facilitates an opportunity for the Holy Spirit to eliminate the mental programming that confines us.

The energy required to perform this is enormous, and at times, it can feel overwhelming. Nevertheless, consistently practicing the "attitude of gratitude," regardless of the images your senses may display, will supernaturally energize both your tenacity and negate the power of the images that once held you captive.

As you continue to embrace the spirit of Thanksgiving, you begin to feel a shift in your attachment to "all things physical." This transformation often accompanies a decrease in the urge to judge. In simpler terms, you'll realize that our tendency to judge is closely linked to our fear of death, stemming from the belief that we need to protect the reflection we see in a mirror.

Reading this may frighten some because they still aren't convinced they are spirits. In fact, many people believe that because God gave them a body and soul, they are meant to rule and reign in a physical state until Jesus arrives to take them home.

This mindset is strengthened by religion and inspired by the wisdom in this dimension. I was taught this and before I explored the teachings of Jesus, I was quick to judge those who held different views.

Only the Holy Spirit can transform our mindset and beliefs, which is the cornerstone of being led by His Spirit.

Your journey starts when you establish a covenant with Christ. This relationship requires you to do nothing until you see His kingdom and find rest. This profound posture introduces you to the spiritual realm, where all things are possible for those who know Him.

Once we recognize that we are more than just physical beings, our connection to fear dissipates. After I chose not to let external factors provoke a fearful reaction, my life changed significantly. However, when it did happen, I simply took a step back from the emotion and consciously shifted my attention to the eternal present moment.

Each physical interaction we have throughout eternity peels away layers of our false sense of security, ultimately revealing our true origins and purposes. We should not be misled into thinking that our personal revelations in the spiritual dimensions should be shared unless directed to do so by the Holy Spirit. This is to ensure we detach our reliance on this realm for validation or praise and instead rely solely on the unseen realm and His voice.

There are many distractions, and our mindset resists any change that could prevent us from making decisions that undermine our control. However, you will quickly learn that nothing in this dimension offers greater peace or joy than staying present.

For many of us, the main challenge—aside from being present—is the constant stream of thoughts and feelings triggered by our dependence on physical stimulation. The ongoing drama we once thought was random seems relentless. However, by enhancing our gratitude, we can reduce both the frequency and impact of these distractions, ultimately fostering peace in our lives.

We will realize that our desires to promote drama for protecting our image undermine peace, leading us to lose interest and remain present instead.

Humanity was freely given the authority to create, allowing them to manifest the same love on earth that originated within the Father. Nevertheless, God was aware of man's inevitable choices and separation, yet He was confident in Christ to fulfill His redemption plan, which makes our position of thanksgiving so powerful.

In other words, recognizing that our end was completed before time or flesh existed embodies the mindset required to surrender ourselves in trust, believing that each day unfolds within His love for us. Our gratitude signifies this awareness, generating a frequency that elevates us beyond our senses and thoughts.

The moments we spend observing our reactions to our physical surroundings yield incredible insights that the Holy Spirit uses to remind us of our origin in Him, which places us in the heavenly dimensions.

I noticed very early while remaining present that much of my day revolved around preserving and enhancing a fabricated image of myself, which lacked real substance and merely provided a deceptive sense of control over future circumstances. These insights have helped me recognize the energy I was wasting maintaining this illusion has been used to expand my understanding and revelation of Christ.

Our spiritual being has no image, nor does it exist outside of Christ and His Word, which was the design from the beginning. However, our free will and desire to experience this dimension through our senses created a separation from the oneness of our origin.

Image is the root of imagination and a gift from God to enhance man's understanding of his spiritual origin. I have had visions of heavenly beings during worship that encourage me beyond words to pursue the love emanating from those visitations.

However, sharing those images with others gave me a false feeling of superiority and removed the essence of the spiritual encounter, which was to release thanksgiving and profound joy.

Today, I inspire others to personally embrace the joy of the Lord and His encounters as a unique gift from their Heavenly Father. Value it as you would a cherished moment with your spouse. My commitment to this practice has helped me remain connected to the unseen and the present moment for longer durations.

A key message of this book is that entering into a covenant with Christ starts with receiving the gift of salvation. However, this is only the beginning! We then need to actively seek and embrace the kingdom of God as renewed citizens.

Can you see the beauty of God's design through His covenants? We truly are the New Testament, and the incredible power to create heaven on earth is found in the oneness we hold within the ark that embodies our essence and beauty. Nothing is impossible, and I'm sure you already know that!

YOU ARE **THE NEW** TESTAMENT

CONCLUSION

We originate from within God as spiritual creators before becoming flesh with free will, which initially produces a divine longing to reconnect with our Creator.

The Bible provides guidance in this quest, addressing our profound need for connection. Its scriptures, inspired by the Holy Spirit, lead Jesus to advocate for our rebirth, which necessitates a shift in our mindset and the acknowledgment of our identity as spiritual beings.

Without this transformation, we will interpret the Bible's words through worldly wisdom, which we recognize as an anti-Christ spirit. This spirit is subtle and always leads to destruction. This highlights why Jesus manifested as the Holy Spirit and why our covenant with Christ is the most crucial aspect in discovering the hidden treasures within us.

> *"However, the helper, the Holy Spirit, whom the Father will send in My name, will teach you everything. He will remind you of everything that I have ever told you."*
>
> John 14:26 GWT

Understanding our spiritual origins starts with recalling that God's Bible is Christ, and unless the Spirit leads us, the Bible today will conceal that truth.

The current Bible was compiled by men without the guidance of the Holy Spirit, reflecting a mindset limited to this dimension, starting with the greatest deception, namely the separation between the Old and New Testaments.

Furthermore, the arrangement of the books and the inclusion of chapters and verses ensure that understanding them requires the Holy Spirit's interpretation. I do not claim that the scriptures lack divine inspiration; rather, I emphasize that they cannot be fully comprehended through our earthly mindset.

Jesus' fulfillment of the Law ended the temporary covenants we discussed and fulfilled God's prophecy in Genesis 3:15.

> *"He will crush your head, and you will bruise His heel."*
>
> Genesis 3:15

That fulfillment marked the beginning of God's eternal covenants, offering salvation to all mankind by replacing salvation through the Mosaic Law and opening His kingdom to everyone reborn of His Spirit and water.

Paul's letters in the "New Testament" form the basis of modern church teachings on salvation through grace. However, these letters are often misinterpreted as guidelines for constructing physical sanctuaries, which God abolished in 70 AD.

Instead, God's intention was to dwell within His creation rather than in a building, allowing humanity to embody His living New Testament.

Paul's mission to the Gentiles necessitated a tabernacle for preaching the gospel of grace, but that was specific to that time. Additionally, Paul's followers view salvation by grace as God's greatest gift.

I believe this stems from the current structure and division of the Bible, which is why Jesus emphasized to His disciples the importance of His transition to the Holy Spirit to impart His teachings to those in Him before the foundation of the world.

The transformative message of salvation through grace is only the beginning, which is why Jesus commanded us to seek His Kingdom, starting with a New Birth.

His resurrection ushers in the covenant of covenants, shaping our identity as His New Testament and bringing forth increasingly profound revelations across generations. The power of this spiritual covenant will empower you as His living testament, revealing the teachings He shared with His disciples during the forty days following His resurrection.

The real power of the Bible lies not in its structure or presentation, but in the individual it represents. The remarkable transformation from Jesus of Nazareth to The Christ should inspire us all to recognize that we are designed to exist fully as both physical and spiritual beings.

Notably, when we recognize that Jesus has fulfilled His mission, the first insight we gain is that we are living in eternity now because we are seated with Him. In other words, His death and resurrection transformed the very fabric of time itself, reminding us that He is, was, and will always be. This means we perceive everything around us as God's perfect design and will.

The Bible consists of God's spiritual words made tangible through His covenants. These covenants were initiated over time and evolved through generations, culminating in the birth, death, and resurrection of Christ—events that occurred beyond this space-time continuum.

A remarkable attribute of the Bible is the Holy Spirit's ability to patiently wait to reveal insights from the spiritual realm, as He did for me by taking me to my origin to validate my covenant with Christ. This profoundly convinced me that the Bible was never meant to be separated into the Old and New Testaments.

Until we experience the new birth that Jesus explained to Nicodemus, our lives will remain unchanged, like so many of those who came before us, waiting for something from outside to alter the treasure that already resides within our spirit.

The quickest way to understand the depth of our somnambulist state is through conscious awareness. This simple yet profound practice will reveal the extent of hypnotic conditioning we have experienced since birth. Furthermore, merely practicing being present connects us to the eternal present moment, which is the source of faith.

This practice will result in a significant transformation in our prayer life, health, and perception, thereby expanding our understanding beyond this dimension and enabling us to remain in the presence of the risen Christ.

> *But there are also many other things which Jesus did—so vast a number indeed that if they were all described in detail, I suppose that the world itself could not contain the books that would have to be written.*
>
> John 21:25 WEY

In the verse above, John reminds us of the untold treasures that remain hidden—actions performed by

Christ before His ascension that were never recorded. The reason for this is so that He can reveal them to each one of us with whom He establishes a covenant. These truths are what He uses to build the most profound temple within those He chose before the foundation of the world.

This dimension contains nothing we did not observe in Him as spirit. The authority derived from that understanding will surpass the limitations of this dimension and render fear ineffective.

Adam's sin stripped us of our identity as spirit, imposing a sin consciousness that all humanity inherits at birth. Our covenant with Christ empowers us as the last Adam while in this physical body with one significant change.

Adam's sin opened his eyes to focus on the material realm; our covenant with Christ opens our spiritual eyes to the wonders of His kingdom all around us.

The full significance of this transition is not fully comprehensible until it occurs. However, one truth remains: those in Him before the world never left that position. Were you in Him? I think so. How about you?

THE BEGINNING

If you enjoyed this book, we also recommend

Immersed In Him

Imagine yourself completely free from fear, disease, and death. Now ask yourself, would your life be any different today if that imagination was the truth? What if this book ripped away the veil of darkness hiding that reality from you? This book will not only tear away the cloak but also shatter the lies many have believed for centuries.

You will discover the true meaning of "The Living Water" and the profound truths hidden in baptism. This book will impart amazing revelations that will change sickness to health and death to life. You were designed to be an overcomer, not to be overcome. "Nothing is impossible to those who drink from Him and become Immersed In Him."

Available on Amazon and our online store

www.voiceofthelight.com

If you enjoyed this book, we also recommend

The Last Adam

Get ready because the veil that has hidden your true nature and identity is about to be ripped off of you forever! And the gospel preached by the last Adam is the power for your transformation. This isn't a how-to book to improve your current status. It's the key that will unlock what you already knew before the foundation of the world. Do you want to reclaim what Adam lost?

Man was created in the image of the One who created all things. The last Adam was not only resurrected over death, but He also defeated the fear of it. If you've ever been afraid it's because you haven't been told the truth about your true identity. Today, when you hear His voice, take that first step into overcoming fear forever. That's what the last Adam gave us. Now, the choice is yours - but you need to take it!

Available on Amazon and our online store

www.voiceofthelight.com

If you enjoyed this book, we also recommend

The Resurrection Generation

The Resurrection Generation is an experience outside time and space to a dimension to see who you are and where you reside. You were chosen "in" Christ before there was a physical dimension, but what does that mean and how can I regain that position? The answers to those questions will not just change your life, but will open doors to experience life without the fear of death.

The people who read this book will be healed and delivered of every disease associated with this dimension. Why? The identity you portray is susceptible to the consciousness of this world's system, whose foundation is the fear of death. But the real you lives in divine health, free from fear. The fear of death is the link between man's addiction to everything that brings physical death. The Resurrection Generation is the vaccine for the real epidemic that started in the Garden of Eden. Once you are reacquainted with who you are before the foundation of the world the peace that passes all understanding opens your eyes and ears to the sights and sounds of your origin.

Available on Amazon and our online store

www.voiceofthelight.com

If you enjoyed this book, we also recommend

Who Has Bewitched You?

There is nothing more important than the crucifixion and resurrection of Jesus Christ. It is what defines the superiority of Christianity over every other religion in the world. This book will expose you to the greatest witchcraft ever perpetuated in the Church, which is the mixing of truth with lies. There is no doubt Jesus was resurrected, but to twist the fact that He was in the earth 3 days and 3 nights, by celebrating Good Friday and Easter Sunday, takes away the accuracy and power of every prophetic scripture written about Him as our Messiah. When one's conscience compromises to adapt the Truth to tradition, we also break the shield against deception. This is not just any book, it is the most powerful weapon you will ever need to unlock the prophetic in the Bible, to dismantle any lie and to live by His Truth. You will have the key to the mysteries of God hidden for generations.

Available on Amazon and our online store

www.voiceofthelight.com

Recommended Video Series by Emerson Ferrell

www.voiceofthelight.com

Watch us on **Frequencies of Glory TV** and **YouTube**
Follow us on **Instagram**

www.frequenciesofglorytv.com
www.youtube.com/@VoiceoftheLight
www.instagram.com/anamendezferrell

If you really want to be transformed, don't stumble across hundreds of confusing revelations on social media. Experience daily revelation and inspiration, without ads, distractions, or confusing messages. Visit our website today and begin to advance your spiritual life in Christ!

"Daily Manna"
with Ana Méndez Ferrell

"Be Still and Know"
with Emerson Ferrell

Voice of The Light Ministries
P.O. Box 3418
Ponte Vedra, FL. 32004 USA
904-834-2447

www.voiceofthelight.com

www.ingramcontent.com/pod-product-compliance
Lightning Source LLC
Chambersburg PA
CBHW070534170426
43200CB00011B/2419